Dimensions of Thought

Dimensions of Thought

Current Explorations in Time, Space, and Knowledge

Volume I

Produced under the Direction
of Tarthang Tulku

Edited by Ralph H. Moon
and Stephen Randall

Dharma Publishing

PERSPECTIVES ON TSK 1

Line drawings throughout Volumes I and II
by Jenny Pierce Moon

International Standard Book Numbers:
0–913546–77–1; 0–913546–79–8 (paper)

Text in Fototronic Laurel. Display in Fototronic Garamond.
Typeset, printed, and bound by Dharma Press.

9 8 7 6 5 4 3 2 1

To the Growth of Knowledge
throughout Space and Time

Contents

Foreword
Ocean of Knowledge
A Conversation with Tarthang Tulku

I've read parts of *Time, Space, and Knowledge*, although I can't pretend to have understood everything you said. Is this new book, *Dimensions of Thought*, an extension of the previous one?

No, this book isn't intended to be a continuation of the vision. The idea here was not to jump ahead again, but to see what readers of *Time, Space, and Knowledge*, like yourself, are doing with the vision. I wanted to know what has and hasn't been understood, what kind of progress has been made. I also thought it might provide some helpful examples and encouragement for others in their work with *Time, Space, and Knowledge*. The vision does present a challenge to our understanding, and it might be useful for us to try meeting this challenge together.

The material presented here in the form of a single conversation was taken from a number of interviews with and talks given by Tarthang Tulku since the publication of *Time, Space, and Knowledge*. Selection of contents and editing was carried out with assistance from Tarthang Tulku, especially for use in *Dimensions of Thought*.—Ed.

Why is it a "challenge" rather than just a matter of spending time reading and coordinating the ideas in the different sections of the book?

Time, Space, and Knowledge presents a new way of being, growing, and coping. Also, it involves a new approach to understanding, and this poses a fundamental difficulty for the reader.

What is the difficulty? Just becoming accustomed to something new?

That alone can be a considerable hurdle in this case. Basically, any reference to new insights or discoveries may be taken—mistaken—as also including a subtle reference back to the structures of ordinary knowledge. *Time, Space, and Knowledge* has 'experiential' exercises, logical critiques of trends within ordinary knowledge, and discussions of visionary paths. But there remains a tendency for people to interpret them in terms of the 'meanings' and logic fundamental to lower knowledge, which include the knowing subject, known object, act of perception, objective world as common reference point, and so on.

It certainly is hard to get away from the idea that 'knowing' must have something to do with one's head, one's self, with relationships between 'me', 'you', and 'it'.

If 'I', with 'my' consciousness and senses, am not involved, how can we speak of any possibility of knowing? Ordinary knowledge can't think outside of its own pattern or perspective, and so we're left with this apparent dilemma.

But if there's no discoverable way out of this ordinary pattern, aren't we faced with a *real*, unsolvable dilemma?

No. The limitation, the apparent impossibility, is itself only a feature of the *picture* we're using, and of the typical pattern of time resulting from using it. It doesn't bear on any real limit to 'our' capacities.

Is this an example of what is discussed in *Time, Space, and Knowledge* as the "read-out law," the idea that no 'read-out' or presentation of time really binds or determines what must obtain within any other presentation?

Yes, it's the same point. If you realize that all of the features and presuppositions characteristic of a given experience need not dictate—as they usually seem to do—the character of other moments of time, then you can begin to escape the ordinary pattern of time and knowledge. That's when you move into what we called "second level" encounters with time and space. Until that has happened, we should at least remain encouraged in exploring new approaches to knowledge.

There is nothing truly paradoxical about a 'knowingness' which both ranges over and draws its support directly from space and time without being limited to a particular knower and known content. The time-space-knowledge vision—especially when used in combination with a continuing critique of the framework of ordinary knowledge—should be sufficient to stimulate more knowingness, clearing the way for its spontaneous emergence. This knowingness can be very immediate, vital, and accurate, without being restricted to sensory and conceptual types of knowledge.

Can it be truly helpful even though it does not relate to the self-oriented picture and cannot be possessed by any 'self'?

Actually, when knowingness *is* made to conform to the logic of ordinary knowledge and perception—so that the self can grasp it—its tangible, beneficial quality is diminished rather than increased. Ordinary knowledge is structured by the seductive, scattering effect of lower time. It is compounded out of past references and future expectations—both encouraging repetition. It's not fresh and keenly sensitive to the present, but rather is always attempting to capture it, to make it conform to approximations and analogies based on recollections. It seems so vital and relevant to us, but it is not really very 'in touch' after all.

So, as we explore the vision and perform the exercises, we must be willing to allow the notion of our 'exploring' and 'doing' something to open into a more fluid kind of knowing?

Yes, otherwise it will be difficult to make any real progress—

—which actually means transcending even the idea of 'progress'?

That's right. Knowingness must be completely limpid, thoroughly open and free of structuring boundaries and strategies. As long as our knowing has such boundaries —even in the case of the more visionary, second level knowledge—it will only present us with specific insights, discoveries, and observations. But true 'knowingness' is not terminated that way; it is absolutely open, embracing without grasping or fixing on something. Ordinary knowledge is always restricted in scope and tainted by its connection to a 'knowing subject'. Things are 'pointed out', but their significance and character reflect the strained, fragmented nature of our approach to knowing them.

Does even the slightest vestige of a 'self', continuity of personal identity framed in terms of past history, and so on, distort knowingness and limit its capacity to give a valid report?

Yes, and the same applies for attempts to avoid these things. For instance, we might try to get away from the 'knowing self', 'acts of knowledge', self as agent or doer, and so on, by trying the opposite—by 'not doing', or becoming passive. In that case we'd still be stuck in the ordinary picture. Rather, the idea should be to not add *or* subtract anything from the immediacy of any knowing encounter. Generally, we are always engaged in such 'adding' just by our insistence on isolating particular items and entities out of any presentation of time. Once we opt for ordinary knowledge in this way, lower time gives us a serial confirmation of the 'thingness' of the items we selected out.

What do you mean by that?

Subsequent moments of time are then constrained to exhibit the 'same things' again, in new positions and relationships. They acquire solidity and continuity.

And there's really an alternative to that typical unfolding of time?

Oh, time can go any way. Remember, one read-out or presentation of time doesn't really bind or dictate the content or character of any other read-outs. Suppose we're back in the initial moment or encounter. If we are more patient—less inclined to jump to premature conclusions in accommodating what is given there—the higher time will reveal a much more profound depth and significance to what is encompassed by our knowing.

Is that where the second level experience of space comes in?

Yes, this is more like what we really mean by *space*. It is not a static emptiness, like the inside of a jug. To understand space you have to appreciate more of time and its penetrating energy.

And to do that you have to find a new approach to knowledge, one that involves neither 'doing' nor 'not doing'.

Right.

But "neither doing nor not-doing" sounds frustratingly elusive, even valueless to the ear of ordinary knowledge. Someone might very naturally consider such talk to be just a play of words, empty distinctions.

Such knowledge remains barred from seeing any road to the acquisition of the structureless, effortless higher knowledge. And by "valueless," do you mean that even if the apparent barrier were overcome and the insight won, it still wouldn't seem worthwhile?

Well, the whole notion of value or worth is ordinarily couched in terms of reference to the self, with its needs and goals. If higher knowledge is not within the range of the self, presents nothing *to* the self, then even if its presence were exposed somehow, it would—almost by definition—be utterly valueless.

What that really suggests is that we should begin to reexamine our ordinary criteria for value. Does our insistence on relating everything to our 'self' succeed in achieving satisfaction, freedom from a temporal series which presents future successors to our present 'knowing self' who still find that they remain off balance, unable to cope, frustrated, in pain? If not, then we may doubt that the self's ability to decide what is valuable or useful is really adequate.

But why would the self willingly miss or shut out something that could be so liberating?

"Willingly" is not quite accurate. It's not a conscious decision or choice.

Even so, the self does seem fundamentally opposed to allowing more knowingness to shine through.

Yes, and the reason is that ordinary knowledge can't recognize what 'we' or our true 'selves' really are. Even if an occasional glimpse of insight into our fundamental nature surfaces, we are not stabilized in that realization, because ordinary knowledge is subject to the essentially unstable, unpredictable wanderings of lower time. So we cannot rest confident and secure in our nature, our 'knowingness'. Our real self is perfect 'knowing', but the ego—due to its insecurity and fearful insistence on getting something solid and meaningful with which it can surround itself—actually does not *want* to be that secure knowingness. Driven by feelings of need and inadequacy, we would rather mistakenly identify ourselves with impotent, but concretely defined, shadows than acknowledge our primordial nature. Any tendency toward the taking and consolidating of positions is due to a subtle misunderstanding of our relationship to the openness of space and the unlimited, expressive play of time—

—and it contributes, in turn, toward deepening such misunderstanding?

Right, because static, rigid positions and identities are easily threatened by such openness and free expression. A chain reaction can therefore easily occur, in which even a subtle inclination toward taking positions can be the decisive turning point, fully sufficient to lead to the development of all the features of lower knowledge. Such a development is thoroughly arbitrary and artificial for the important reason that it needlessly disguises and leads us away from our Being.

This reminds me that some people feel you try to go too far in *Time, Space, and Knowledge*. They say that you at-

tempt to extend logical critiques and analyses into areas beyond their proper sphere of application—in short, that there's no way to effectively criticize ordinary knowledge or to get any satisfactory answer concerning such fundamental issues as our "Being."

In *Time, Space, and Knowledge* we encourage sustained critiques and analyses, and simultaneously point out the limitations of using ordinary logic and analysis to obtain truly fundamental insights. We are simply urging the use of ordinary analysis only up to the point where we can see, if we're being honest with ourselves, the need for (and at least the faint possibility of) yielding up the limiting postures of such knowledge and analysis. This is a way of preparing to open to higher knowledge.

But then other people feel that, by insisting on the limitations of ordinary knowledge, you are taking an anti-intellectual and prematurely despairing position.

Actually, what we've said is that whether a satisfactory answer is available or not depends on the position we take, on the kind of knowledge we use, and that ordinary knowledge and logical investigation are sufficient for a good beginning, as long as we don't follow them in a rigid way. The most important point is that we should not get stuck in *any* position—either for or against the capabilities of ordinary knowledge—that limits our ability to accommodate new possibilities, to broaden our base for appreciating space and time. After all, the one thing that ordinary knowledge shows us beyond any doubt is that humanity is still burdened by ignorance, by a lack of an-

swers to crucial problems. If we shut down or limit our
development as knowing beings, what chance will we
have? We are in a position now to review and assess the
achievements of our culture through several thousand
years of history. How are we doing? ·

We've made vast progress in many areas.

True, but still there's been little fundamental change
in our lot as human beings; the basic issues of human
existence remain as a challenge to our insight and our
willingness to initiate a qualitative change in our nature as
conscious inhabitants of the universe.

**Certainly some thinkers would agree with that. Although
they may not have been talking about what you call
"higher knowledge" as being essential, people have interpreted history as showing that any amount of progress—
when restricted to the level of ordinary perception and
mentation, of subject-object duality—will fail to address
the basic problem of attaining complete harmony in our
lives and society. It is also interesting to note that if we
take recorded history as a test sample from which we
might make some predictions, the only thing we can predict *with certainty* is that we'll get ourselves into more
trouble and conflict.**

Yes, there will be a repetition of those familiar trends
and features of life which, taken together, constitute what
we call "suffering" or "unsatisfactoriness." Your point
about prediction is interesting because lower time and
knowledge are exactly like that. The time is unstable and

cannot support peace and security for long. Knowledge is weak, uncertain in reading what time will bring. We can predict very little about the positive aspects of life—

—except that they will be infrequently enjoyed and quick to fade.

Right. Such certainty of suffering, and uncertainty regarding practically everything else, is not accidental or meaningless. It must be taken as relevant evidence in our attempt to evaluate ordinary knowledge.

So what do you conclude?

Just that in this case, history does show us an aberration rather than simply a 'normal' but regrettable state of affairs. We can conclude that our knowledge to date is not—*but should be*—unbounded. It is always bound, circumscribed, taking limiting positions in time and space as its point of departure, and then—as lower time follows its tortuous path from there—acquiring and preserving more and more binding restrictions, positions. The resulting knowledge or awareness is actually constituted by this characteristic pattern of time; it doesn't possess any notion of another way of relating to time.

As we were saying, by its very nature it sees no escape?

Worse still, it refuses to permit any critique or investigation of its own foundations in search of an alternative. This is why it's natural to find objections to *Time, Space, and Knowledge*'s critiques of ordinary time and knowledge. This kind of knowledge wants to preserve itself as the only possibility, even in the midst of its inevitable companion, suffering. There is a kind of sad humor in the fact that this total lack of choice, this total absence of alternatives, is itself something that has been unconsciously chosen and rigorously defended by ordinary knowledge.

We need a more survival-oriented approach, one that, in its relationship with the power of time, provides us with more confidence and balance, with a more predictably healthy existence. But this would mean directly confronting time's energy, something which seems both threatening and elusive to the 'self'. We, our 'selves', demand a solution that is sufficiently staid and concrete to appease our fears. We insist on something that has a specific form, on a type of knowing that we can possess, on *content*. This insistence, in turn, leaves us back where we started, with no viable alternative, and so we repeat ourselves continually.

Is there any limit to this cycle?

Well, in one way there's no limit, because time is infinite. But we are building very fragile structures in time, and since this cycle not only repeats itself but also escalates in intensity, we and our structures do have a definite limit. Eventually, the pressures built up within our crowded space by a driving, uncontrollable time may become more than our knowledge can handle. At that point, survival fails.

Are we now arriving at such a point?

I cannot say, but we must decide soon whether or not we are willing to see the pattern of time we've initiated through to its natural conclusion. By using time, space, and knowledge we can discover security and fulfillment within Being.

Is that a way of saying that we can live up to our human potential, that in fact we can no longer afford to ignore the full range of possibilities in our 'human being'?

Yes, we commonly refer to it as "potential," our human potential. But actually, it is not merely *potential*. It is already radiating throughout our lived existence. It is the very basis of our lived existence. By acknowledging this potential, we achieve fulfillment within our own nature, while by ignoring it we pursue a powerfully divisive, self-destructive path. The time-space-knowledge vision shows us a way back to ourselves. It can make a great contribution, but only if we explore it without interpreting it in terms of the models and familiar patterns of ordinary knowledge, and without drawing premature conclusions regarding its message and methods.

Generally, we want to fit a new idea into our own conceptual schemes, to tailor it to our individual styles and goals.

It's fine to try to use *Time, Space, and Knowledge* to enhance your own interests and styles, but you mustn't turn it into an extension of your pattern of ordinary knowledge. If you interpret it that way, it just becomes a mere duplication or variation of existing concepts, lacking the power to help in any fundamental way. Perhaps more than anything else, it is important for us to practice investigating and expanding our knowledge and the additions to knowledge suggested in *Time, Space, and Knowledge* without taking fixed positions about the limits and possibilities of knowledge or drawing premature conclusions about the meaning of what we discover along our path to Being.

Are you then trying to protect the separate integrity of the vision as a specific doctrine, to keep people from changing the ideas?

No, that's not my point.

But it seems as though here and in the book *Time, Space, and Knowledge* you make sharp critiques of any ideas or approaches that differ from the vision.

It may *seem* as though we are criticizing competing views, but that's really not at all what we're saying. What we're trying to do is to support intelligent progress, any kind of new developments, as long as they are truly *new*. The critiques are just intended to cut away or warn against those tendencies and presuppositions that attach themselves to our thinking and then channel our attempts at progress back into familiar, repetitive patterns.

Will you permit critiques of the vision itself then, as long as the critiques assist progress in truly new directions?

It's not for me to permit or reject other people's criticisms or developments, but yes, I absolutely agree that we should investigate the time-space-knowledge vision in that way. The only thing we're trying to *defend* is *intelligence*, in the widest possible sense. The vision is in itself just a step, not a doctrine. We want intelligence to be liberated so that it can begin to work independently, without duplications, even if this means going beyond some hypothetical duplication someone might find in *Time, Space, and Knowledge*. We're looking for *complete* independence of thought.

That seems impossible, even meaningless. Our thought must be a reflection of our cultural heritage, our intellectual environment. Thought can't exist on its own, without the support of a wider background of significance—without a touchstone.

I agree, but we can find a better, less limiting touchstone than the one we're using now. The 'knowledge' component of the vision is not 'thinking in a vacuum'; it's an honest acknowledgement of an open-ended reality. Each person's thinking can become free of the restrictions of any 'outside influence' and still be accurate, well founded.

It still seems difficult. Also, such a multiplicity of views would result that you'd have chaos.

No, it only seems that way if you interpret this independence from within the presuppositions of ordinary knowledge. But complete individual freedom is not incompatible with objectivity and universal harmony. Don't be afraid. Go as far as you can, even if it means going beyond the present vision, as long as your 'knowing' is securely grounded in its attention to time and space.

So, would it be fair to say that the book *Time, Space, and Knowledge* and its vision are still first and second level views, but the real ti... , space, and knowledge are something further, constituting a third level?

It's true that there is a kind of time-space-knowledge vision you can find beyond what is described in the book, the stated vision. But, if you look carefully, you'll see that in a subtle way even the higher vision is present there, in the explicit statement. At least, nothing is missing from the book that you need in order to progress to the higher vision. This is especially important. You have everything you need in *this* 'step', *Time, Space, and Knowledge*. There is no truth or realization that's in principle beyond your reach. It's not as though you lack some secret mantra or initiation, or that you're completely cut off from reality by your cultural conditioning, and so on.

And the same applies to personal weaknesses, psychological limitations, or guilt about past actions—they don't block me from making progress?

If you think about such things in the ordinary way they can cause problems, but they cannot take away your chance, especially when you apply the time-space-knowledge vision to your situation. This is the vision's special gift. It promotes real love and healing within yourself; you don't need to feel tainted or flawed. So, in this way true freedom can develop. It's not a feeling of relief or exhilaration because someone has done a ceremony over you, absolving you of your sins.

Again, we're talking about promoting a more active *intelligence.* When you can see directly that you and everything about you are space and knowledge, then time has nothing to bind anymore, so there's no "karma," if you want to use a word like that. Don't rely on other people to save you. Make your own knowledge direct and powerful. When you look at traditional religious teachings, you see that the highest level of such teachings always directs the emphasis back—"God is within you."

But these messages have been simplified and misunderstood—

—interpreted by ordinary knowledge again—

—so instead of promoting self-sufficiency, they become mysteries. "Within you" is taken to mean "within the 'self'," so you get a picture of God, an omnipotent Self of some kind, secretly hiding inside our self-image. This is much too simple.

On the other hand, what you've been saying in *Time, Space, and Knowledge,* **going beyond the idea of a self, even beyond 'salvation', seems so subtle that people will wonder what good the vision is—***for whom* **is it good?**

But, again, those problems arise because the interpretations are too simplistic, too much a duplication of old patterns. When we learn to think in a truly new way, the love, healing, and self-reliance we were talking about can arise without our objecting, "*Who* is healed?" and without our interpreting self-reliance as reliance on a self-image, or lower knowledge.

If the higher levels of some other traditions are trying to transmit a similar insight, are you really saying anything new?

In one way, we're not saying anything new because all scientific, religious, and psychological disciplines are confronting space and time, too—what else, at bottom, is there for them to explore? However, the problem with at least some of these other approaches is that they are investigating space and time very indirectly and unconsciously rather than directly and intentionally. Such an approach can yield insights and benefits for a while, but it is very slow, and capable of being exhausted. Since it's not aware of the real basis of its object of study, this approach can become frozen into artificial, static models.

So you feel we need a more direct approach, and *Time, Space, and Knowledge* suggests an example of what that might be like?

Yes, it's at least a beginning. It is really our duty to confront and accept the dynamic principles that are reflected in the universe around us. Science, through the centuries, has performed a valuable function by debunking the simplistic anthropocentrism characteristic of ordinary knowledge. The self is not the center of the universe.

But in a way, knowledge or knowingness, and we as intelligent beings, are in a kind of central position with respect to the forces and dramatic developments occurring everywhere around us. It is really our role to become conscious witnesses and participants. By far the greatest part of such a confrontation remains to be attempted. Neither the cave paintings of our ancestors nor the most sophisticated modern telescopes are sufficient for accomplishing such a task. The tools and modes of thought we've been using so far are too limited. It may become increasingly difficult to make major, fundamental discoveries using such tools.

Similarly, in the sphere of human interactions, it may become difficult to remain in touch with each other, to develop new and effective social structures and social harmonies, because we are not in touch with our own natures. Without more 'knowingness', we can't contact and savor the deep 'flavor' of our own present experience. As a consequence, we lack the basis for sharing our lives and experiences with each other. In the long run, this could lead to our losing our 'humanity'.

Time, space, and knowledge are offering us so much, but we ignore the possibilities. We limit ourselves to a very superficial, transitory expression of 'human being'. It's as though we were mining for ore, but using clumsy tools or looking in the wrong places. The greatest treasure that was ever available to mankind is still perfectly preserved within space, and still available to us, not for us to *own* as isolated individuals, but for us to share and enjoy together, in a way that *contributes* to the universe rather than taking from it.

Let's excavate time, space, and knowledge! By doing this, we can support our supporter; for time, space, and knowledge have been providing support throughout the ages. We've been short-sightedly drawing from these reservoirs, appropriating their resources for our own selfish purposes. But this has proved rather silly and self-defeating. We're losing ground rather than gaining it in this game.

Let's try it the other way for awhile, recognizing the support of space and time, and committing ourselves to the priorities and imperatives we discover within a deeper knowledge. Knowledge preserves a kind of open channel between us and space and time, so the basis for sharing the deeply satisfying qualities they bear still exists. In this way, we can develop a way of life beyond the usual rushing from day to night, moment to moment. We don't have to try to squeeze fulfillment out of the measured portions of time we find in the 'past', 'present', and 'future'. There is a time that is not divided into such limited points.

The freedom that this higher knowledge brings us—a freedom in relating to time and space—is far greater than the freedom afforded by yards or miles of extra space, by greater quantities of natural resources, by technological advances and 'time-saving' devices. Also, this freedom cannot be enjoyed by a few people to the detriment of the majority: if you have it, you automatically share it. Humanity can finally be united.

Don't traditional religions talk about this same possibility of uniting mankind through love?

They do, but love must involve this higher knowledge, otherwise your attempt at unification will fail.

Why?

Because to work for others, to share and participate in life freely with them, you must see directly that you and they are the same. Your bodies are the same space, if you probe deeply enough. Your energies are all drawn from the same time. Your experiences and aspirations are all ways of using the same knowledge, and remain unified within that knowledge. We have never moved apart from one another, never become different or separate beings. Until we see this directly, how can we feel real compassion for our fellow human beings? We might have feelings and make gestures motivated by cultural conditioning, guilt, or sentimentality, but an unconditional compassion must come from deep knowledge. Then we can all explore the vastness and beauty of space and time together.

And such an exploration would not become a selfish hoarding of sensations, because we wouldn't *be* selfish?

More than that—there wouldn't be any way for you to remain a mere enjoyer, soaking up and sharing pleasures. You would necessarily be an active participant, holding back nothing of yourself. There *is* no solid self. You are an open-ended expression of time, space, and knowledge. Ideally, you draw whatever you need from space and time, but also give everything that you are back, by acknowledging your unity with them. It's a spontaneous, simultaneous exchange. By comparison, ordinary 'human being', in which our Being is obscured, is a very mechanical process. Our reactions are practically of the 'knee jerk' variety, and we're motivated by a small set of needs, predicated on insecurity and lack of fulfillment. The result is a long history of actions that are essentially repetitive in nature, nothing very new.

From the way you're talking, it sounds almost as though our efforts at progress are being sabotaged.

Why is that?

Well, according to what you say, even our ordinary way of life and history are an expression of time, space, and knowledge. Why are they acting in this frustrating, repetitive way?

Time, space, and knowledge do not act in one particular way, this one or any other. But it's a matter of how deeply we acknowledge our connection with them. Whether we acknowledge them or not, we are using them, *and they are using us.* Just because we ignore them, depending on them only unconsciously, doesn't mean that there's no interchange. We are still bound to time and space; we and they are inseparable companions. If we ignore our connection to them, we relegate ourselves to lives of a kind of menial, trivial service: the only way we allow ourselves to be used by the universe at large.

But one way or another, we will be used?

Yes, it's impossible to completely cut ourselves off from the process of give-and-take.

How does this relate to what you said earlier about a great treasure being preserved for us within space? Is it all just a matter of what we "acknowledge"?

Yes.

Why should that make such a difference? Whether we recognize reality to be, fundamentally, one thing or another, it doesn't seem to change what we encounter and experience on an ordinary, day-to-day level very much.

"Acknowledging" is not just an acceptance of an *idea*. Remember, the emphasis is on active expression—*participation*. What is the depth and quality of our participation?

Imagine that you live within the depths of an 'ocean'; you are completely permeated by it. It gives to you, and you take what it offers, acting in ways that are expressive of the purity and power of the water. The results of your actions remain within that same sphere, flowing freely back into the water. But the 'ocean' is vast, unbridled power, not limited or constrained by anything, and constrains nothing. It permits everything, even ways of relating to it that are very limited and 'stand-offish'.

Let's suppose that you become identified with one of these narrow, aloof ways of interacting with the ocean. It's as though you have drawn above it, ignoring the qualities and depth of its waters. You don't even "acknowledge" that depth; you don't knowingly interact with it. But you can never completely sever your connection, so you can never avoid depending on it and interacting with it in some way. The result is that the ocean leaps up and slaps you in the face with the peaks of its high, jagged waves.

This is the only form of contact your aloof stance will permit.

Perhaps you come to live on the very peaks of these waves and look across to the peaks of other waves around you. You pretend that reality is comprised only of what floats there on the peaks, that there is no 'underneath', not even any supporting water, except perhaps in some abstract sense. Even so, part of your new existence is the constant, shocking sensation of being struck by ocean sprays.

Perhaps you take this unpleasant experience as meaningless, just a 'background phenomenon'. But it won't go away. Always churned about by the waves, out of phase with the rise and fall of other peaks, it is hard to relate satisfactorily to others. The structures you build seem unstable, subject to some relentless, destabilizing power, and you are always struck in the face by the surging water.

If, eventually, you relax your obsession with scanning across the peaks, and become willing to give more attention to the water itself, to acknowledge it in a participatory sense, you can delve deeply into the ocean. Then, much to your vast amazement, the annoying stinging sprays and the undermining influence of the waves ceases. Your awareness is not restricted to maintaining contact with tiny, erratically jumping objects separated from you by unbridgeable distances.

'Beauty', 'peace', 'security', 'fulfillment', 'intimacy', 'knowledge', 'communication', 'coexistence' all come to acquire meanings very different from what they had for you on the surface. This 'ocean' and its 'waves' are only rough metaphors for the range of space and time as they are seen by different types of knowledge, different degrees of participation. Frustration, loss, and separation may have been typical themes for the knowledge of the surface, which was subject to the waves. But nothing can be lost or exhausted for that knowledge which remains attuned to the depths of space and time. Everything that fulfills and delights, and everything that stimulates knowledge to become more sensitive and encompassing, is perfectly preserved there. You can see why it's so important that we be totally 'in' or 'within' time, space, and knowledge.

But it sounds like this "within" amounts to a deep *immersion* in some medium, an absorption of the self in a substratum.

No, the metaphor of the ocean shouldn't be taken that far. The self is not becoming entangled in something or being absorbed into something else: it is already time, space, and knowledge. This central fact simply needs to become more visible. In this way, our knowledge becomes more open and responsive, rather than being intoxicated with some otherworldly absolute. We become better able to accommodate and cope with our reality.

Including the peaks of the waves in your example?

Exactly. Even within the apparent wave or surface phenomena you can find this liberating quality. The tangle of happenings still remains completely part of the ocean's quality. In fact, for higher knowledge there's no discernible 'surface' as opposed to the 'depths'. The freedom of space and time permits certain circumstances to arise, from the viewpoint of one sort of knowledge, in which it seems that 'we' are pitted against the vast power and indifference of the physical universe. But even in such cases, it's actually knowledge itself responding *to* itself. It appears that we are responding to the universe, but actually the universe is responding within itself. However, this does not mean that there is some determinate *thing* or system or natural order responding in one way, or on one level, *to* something; that ordinary picture can't begin to embrace the depth and open-endedness of this participation.

Here, again, our attitude about who or what is responding does make a difference?

Definitely, although it's not exactly an attitude that's involved. If we can see clearly that it's space, time, and knowledge that's involved, rather than 'me', this has the immediate effect of freeing us from tensions, fears, and limiting habits. The one who's angry, sick, or due to confront some unpleasant, frightening situation is really space, time, and knowledge. Think for a minute about the problems you have in the course of a typical day. Try to imagine how you would face those problems if 'you' knew that they were space and time presenting situations to knowledge itself rather than to 'you'.

I can think of some situations where it would make a difference: I might have more confidence in a way, less resistance or timidity. But there also seems to be some-

thing strange and artificial about thinking, "It's not *me* that's doing this; it's something else."

That's true. I said it was not a matter of an attitude or a conceptual shift of some kind. It takes a very carefully prepared, subtle intelligence to understand the meaning of what you paraphrase as, "It's not me." It is easy to misunderstand, in which case it becomes another proposition of ordinary knowledge, stating that some *other* subject or agent is acting, performing in ordinary time. This is not a correct view.

Our whole purpose is to go beyond this typical lower time orientation of 'someone's doing something'. Moreover, this kind of mistake is very dangerous, since it imprisons us even more by blinding us to the immediacy of experience and binding us to what *Time, Space, and Knowledge* called an "outside-stander." If we can understand this correctly, using the knowledge that attends to time and space, then our difficulties in living can be solved very easily, naturally.

Is this comparable to a new form of therapy or a new approach in psychology?

You can use this insight and freedom to make advances in many fields. Psychology is one area where you might apply it, although it would involve a radically new orientation, since *Time, Space, and Knowledge* is not based on modifying or balancing the self-image or its *feelings*. Nor is there any formal *model* of the human being or the mind being proposed here. Our approach to 'mental health' begins on a level where no reference is made to such frozen structures as the 'mind' or 'psyche'.

Could you give me an example of how to develop this subtle understanding?

There are many good approaches discussed in *Time, Space, and Knowledge*, but if you want a simple example of this 'knowing', of 'being within time, space, and knowledge', imagine that you are sitting quietly with your eyes closed.

Is this going to be like the exercises in *Time, Space, and Knowledge*?

No, this isn't an exercise at all. I'm not saying you should actually *do* this in a formal way. Just think about it. See if you can get a 'taste' of this knowledge. Imagine that your eyes are closed; it's very dark. It's as though you're starting your confrontation with reality anew, innocent of ordinary presences like visible light, objects, and so on.

Imagine within that darkness a special kind of light— not like ordinary light—very gentle and illuminating, but not harsh or blinding to the senses. It is almost like space, an open, all-embracing warmth—not an object or thing, but a quality within everything you are and feel. It's extremely important that you don't make this quality an object or a target for the grasping of the ordinary mind. Let it remain as a kind of intermediate presence. It's present, but not as a *thing*.

Now, abide within that. Don't move past it. It's almost like a feeling of pure joy, but you must be careful not to grasp at this joy as something heavy, as an intoxication of pleasure. It must delight and stimulate intelligence rather than bind it.

Now slowly open your eyes, allowing the light quality to be even more open-ended in scope and character, so that it can include all perceived presences within itself. You must be careful not to let awareness be seduced into making subtle transitions into the ordinary mode of drawing apart as the perceiving subject, viewing objects which are discernible to the senses by virtue of being illuminated by ordinary light. Remain with the primary awareness and encompassing presence of 'light'.

If you do lose this quality and stray into the secondary, structured landscape of subjects and objects, the liberating power of time and the open radiance of space are obscured. They become a mystery, beyond the possibility of being located 'somewhere' in space or developed 'somehow' in time. But, if you can stay with the light, you'll find that it is part of all presences, all moments, so the experiences of daily life remain within there, preserving and transmitting the light.

Seeing the great variety of appearance as still bearing the light also provides you with a wider sense of the light's quality. By thus expanding your understanding of the light, you become sensitized to it, so that you can see even more of it, attending to it more deeply. This in turn allows you to 'expand' within it, not by letting 'your awareness' go 'outward' in the directions of ordinary space, but by intensifying the quality itself so it becomes still more encompassing of phenomena. Again, the more it embraces, the more precisely its inner nature is revealed, and so the cycle goes, maturing toward an understanding of the insight we were discussing earlier, the realization that time, space, and knowledge are responding, not 'me'.

In reality, once you open your eyes, even if you approach the field of presences with this kind of open-minded innocence, there will still be ordinary light shining, illumining your surroundings and activating the usual light receptors in your eyes. How can you get past the basic functioning of your senses?

If you open your eyes very carefully, subtly preserving your connection with the more gentle, embracing light, then the light you discover will be very different from the ordinary sort: the radiance and colors will be more like those of a rainbow. Ordinary colors, red, blue, and so on, are very dull and *uninspiring* compared to this rainbow-like cascade. Your senses themselves can work differently if they are using a more open space and a more exhilarating time. Higher knowledge is not something completely ethereal; it includes an expansion and refinement of our ordinary perceptual capacity. You can see all physical substance and form to be manifestations of this subtle but brilliant light.

It sounds like heaven.

It's a heaven that's not 'beyond' in the sense of being elsewhere. You have to expand beyond ordinary perceptions, but 'expand' and 'beyond' simply mean opening to more of the *presence* of the light. You expand within and *as* that light.

The light is so encompassing, so ready to embrace and nourish everything, that it gives a new significance to the idea of 'love'. Much of what we ordinarily call "love" remains on the level of self-centered sensations. But if you relate to people and presences from within that light, love can be truly perfected, not limited to the prejudices and urgencies experienced by the self-image. Everything can be united within the presence of the light as the integration of time, space, and knowledge. But again, it's important that we don't take this 'presence' as 'something present' in the ordinary sense—something 'here' related 'to us', as opposed to something absent, somewhere else. The great beauty we've just mentioned is available precisely because and when there's no audience, when there are no self-images bending it to their purposes, restricting it to their characteristics and capacities for fulfillment.

The only audience is knowingness itself, which does not relate to space and time in such a way that it can be located as an event 'here' in space, in this 'present' interval of time. For that very reason, nothing is excluded from it, everything is *within* it, part of the range of its appreciation. If it assumes any position so as to focus on one aspect of what is 'present' to the exclusion of another aspect, then space and time recede to the background, becoming just a stage on which we perform; we are no longer aware of being *within* them. So we have a situation comparable to the turbulence of the waves obscuring the depth of the ocean again.

Do all of the senses expand and change when we are knowingly 'within' space and time, or is a primarily visual field of knowledge involved?

Hearing, taste, touch—everything opens. The more you are actively 'within', the more your senses and perceptions can accommodate. Such an increase in sensitivity and capacity is like a sign, indicating that your approach is correct and inviting you to go even further.

So that's not necessarily the whole vision yet?

No. It's just the initial unfolding of the vision, a taste.

How does this initial stage relate to traditional religious experience?

Perhaps some traditional religious experience is based on this qualitative explosion in our sensitivities. But it's essential that we guard against getting stuck. We might become infatuated with these visions and signs of development. They may seem vast, even infinite in their beauty and offer of fulfillment, but if we relate to them in a closed way, rather than allowing them to remain within the open-ended embrace of the light, we lose sight of the full scope of time, space, and knowledge. Since, as we were saying, you cannot shut them out and reject their offer of full participation without becoming *subject* to them, this is dangerous as well as being limited.

Being 'within' the light or 'within' time, space, and knowledge seems so important that it makes me a little nervous that I still don't know exactly *how* to do it. Even

your example of closing and then opening the eyes is a little general. Could you give me a precise technique for staying within the primary quality of the light, for not straying into the secondary, frozen presences of subject and object? What do I do first?

Wait, wait . . . [laughs]. That's exactly the problem! The whole idea of a technique is to give the ego, the self-image a *sequence* of lower time moments that it can set into motion—what people properly call a "course of action." This is rather self-defeating if our goal is to open to the immediate *presence* of higher time. Techniques, by their very nature, perpetuate the old view and the problems that result from it. This is why I didn't describe the example of opening the eyes as being a real technique or practice.

Is there no way to prepare for being 'within'?

There is no one *to* prepare, and nothing to do. But I agree that in a way preparation is important.

Why doesn't that inconsistency bother you?

Because it's not inconsistent. What has to be prepared is precisely the insight, initially the attitude, that there's no continuous self who has to do something. There's no continuous mind, despite the apparent continuity of our memories and experience. If that seems like too big a claim to accept, look at our discussions about this in *Time, Space, and Knowledge*, and also the article called "Opening Time" in this volume.

And continuity is an issue here because it invokes the continuation of lower time?

The reason you might have trouble going into the light and abiding there is that 'you' are defined in terms of a long past personal history and projected future life of experience. That continuous identity and personal history seems practically as discrete and solid as the human body itself. So, if you try to go into the immediate presence of the light, the 'you' is this whole story framed in a past-present-future format. 'Going into' involves the same problem: you can't relate directly to the light in that way. Rather than thinking of the mind in terms of its temporal profile and continuity, attend more closely to your presence within and as each present moment of experience, each thought or perception.

So the individual present time moment, taken in isolation from all known predecessor moments and all anticipated successor moments, is very important?

Yes and no. That kind of 'present' moment is still part of the picture integral to lower time, as is the idea of concentrating on such a moment or isolating it in that way. Higher knowledge can't even *find* isolated points of time like that. It's a very artificial approach to 'attending to the immediate presence' of the light. Still, initially, this may be the only way we can look, so we talk about "the present moment." Each such moment permits entry into the totality of space and time, and also contains all the other moments which constitute one's personal history, even the history of all experience in the realm of lower knowledge.

How is that possible?

Unlike our allegedly continuous stream of personal history and experience, space and time are truly continuous. Any presentation of time can be opened, using higher knowledge, to any other presentation because time is like a bridge: it preserves the connection among all of its apparent points. Each point contains all points.

Then there are two ways of contacting one's personal history—by casting about over the range of one's past memories and by abiding within the depth of the present moment—

—of what initially *appears* to be the present moment, right. We need a balanced attention to space and time, or to the light, whichever way you want to say it. This attention or abiding "in the depths" does not result from any forcible entry, any straining or control of either mind or body. It grows naturally within itself, intensifying and opening without effort.

It almost sounds like you're saying, "Do nothing. Wait until it happens someday."

No, it is *already* happening within each moment! Any moment you choose involves the whole process. Do you remember what we said earlier about not adding anything—neither doing nor not-doing? *This* is what was meant. Everything required for contacting freedom and everything required to remain in intimate contact with all 'points' of time is already being done.

Even if you're not aware of it?

The self-liberating process continues even then. Initially, since one form of 'knowing' experiences what it takes to be problems and wants an antidote of some sort, we say, "Yes, that's *lower* knowledge. Don't stray into it and its realm of secondary representation, stay in the primacy of the light." But there are really no 'primary' as opposed to secondary dimensions of experience, nothing 'higher' to know. They are the same, even though when we first grapple with this problem, being confused and upset by the frustrating trends of time and by its relentless *movement*, it seems that we have to improve somehow, to know more, to go to another level.

Once we see that the movement of time is only a subtle trick, that different moments occurring in or establishing different 'locations' in time actually occur and remain within the same time, then we know there is no problem, whether we 'stray' into secondary phenomena or not. We can follow every enchanting gesture of time's play, and still avoid being at time's mercy, swept away. But even when we *don't* know this, there's still no problem, in a way.

Here again I'd like to ask why this deceptive motion of time should be occurring at all. Is it simply a result of the type of knowledge we use?

From an intermediate viewpoint, we must say, as we did earlier, that it occurs *as a result* of lower knowledge taking particular positions in time; so time then 'moves', eroding these positions away to show that they are intrinsically artificial. This account reflects and affirms the idea that something has gone wrong; it speaks to that level of insight.

However, there's nothing really wrong with these 'positions' and this 'distributive' kind of time, even if they do involve only a narrow insight into time's nature. Time is not like a machine, with internal structures constraining it toward a preferred mode of operation. It is utterly boundless, open, and flexible. Nothing is forbidden to it; its lucency permits all varieties of expression. Nor is anyone trying to trick us. Once we see this, we can avoid being trapped and tormented by secondary structures in time because we know that there are no *strictly secondary* structures, and there is no place to stray into or to escape from.

This insight is always being made available to knowledge, naturally and effortlessly, by the interactive play of space and time. In contrast, techniques—attempts to force the issue, to improve, control, or achieve—cannot arrive at this understanding. At first it may be necessary to approach time and knowledge by way of techniques, perhaps locking our attention onto each 'present' moment. But the approach itself *and* its motivating premises have to be surrendered eventually, if we are to be free.

Are you equally opposed to this kind of 'technique orientation' or 'therapeutic approach' in the case of more ordinary goals? Take, for instance, the case of psychology or of psychotherapy again.

This is why I mentioned that one's entire personal history is present within each moment of time. By opening to the space, time, and knowledge available within the moment you can also instantly transform all of the 'past' moments preserved 'there'. The psychotherapeutic approach can take a very long time, sifting through all this past experience, trying to neutralize its negative influence. It also seems likely that the job would remain at least partially incomplete: there would always be some unresolved tensions and conflicts, some residue. This is especially likely, because the psychotherapeutic approach deals with *memories*.

But we can draw closer to our target than that. By using the instantaneous unfolding of time, space, and knowledge, everything—all these moments—can be directly contacted within the 'present' and purified of any negative influence. Earlier we were talking about the possibility of a new psychotherapy based on time, space, and knowledge. Such a discipline would involve radically new premises about methodology as well as different views of the human being.

Not only in this case, but in general, I think the time-space-knowledge approach is important. Ordinarily, we are so concerned about trying to wrestle with lower time, working within the limits of that time. More 'esoteric' traditions try to break out of lower time, although they may call it by another name. In either case, we seek techniques, tools, methods, skills, and information. There is another way, fully contained within what may first appear as the 'present moment'. The perceiver, the thing perceived, the action which presents the object to the perceiver—all are completely contained in the moment, inseparable facets of one presence.

Sometimes we speak about *caring* for ourselves and for each other. If we know how to look, the caring or support is immediately available within each of the moments which combine to constitute our lives. The humble moment, when seen as time, space, and knowledge, is a target worth aiming at. It's the vital center of the universe; if we hit it, we explode everything that prevents fulfillment, attaining everything that fulfills.

If you are right, the time-space-knowledge vision should be of great help to mankind. Is this the principal approach you've selected to benefit others here in the West?

I feel very comfortable working with this vision, but not particularly for that purpose.

You're not trying to benefit other people?

Not exactly.

I don't understand. As a Buddhist lama, trained in the Mahayana tradition, isn't your main concern the welfare of all sentient beings?

I'm not offering the time-space-knowledge vision as an extension of Buddhism or Buddhist goals, although I think it's fully compatible with those goals. But to answer your question, we have to distinguish between the vision and the book, *Time, Space, and Knowledge.* I am responsible for producing the book, but the vision was not really created by anyone. Its appearance at this time was not motivated by any desire, compassionate or otherwise, on my part, but by more 'internal imperatives'.

What do you mean?

It came to the foreground of my attention to assist people's participation in time, space, and knowledge, because such participation produces a qualitative change appealing to knowledge—a kind of new, interesting flavor. We are all part of that knowledge, so in a sense some aspect of us all is working in this direction, enjoying this flavor within itself. It's not that there is a taster tasting something tasty; it's knowledge, all within knowledge.

You weren't trying to restate Buddhist or Nyingma thought?

No, I had no conscious idea or desire of that sort. Buddhism is vast, almost beyond my ability to fathom it all; I wouldn't attempt such a restatement. *Time, Space, and Knowledge* suggests an independent path. If it's similar or parallel to Buddhism in some way, fine, but that's not so important.

Your discussion of the need for more participation and this idea of knowledge working toward a "new flavor" make me a little uneasy. I picture people and their priorities being coordinated and even controlled by a kind of collective consciousness or supermind.

There have been many versions of that idea throughout history, but what time, space, and knowledge offer is the exact opposite—real freedom. The point, as discussed earlier, is that the 'self' or ordinary knowledge is being *used* by time, space, and knowledge, because we have abdicated from any central position and are unaware that we are being channelled along in one rut or track. We don't know of any alternatives. If you participate more in time, space, and knowledge, then you have both the knowledge of choices and the freedom to implement them, because you can control time. In the process of exercising this freedom it is also true that people might act with more mutual understanding and, therefore, more 'in concert', but surely that's not such a bad thing. People, traditions, and disciplines in ordinary knowledge are so often in conflict, undermining one another, that more understanding and coordinated action seem like a change in the right direction.

I know some people find *Time, Space, and Knowledge* itself to be so complicated that it seems to be conflicting at times.

The *vision* is the essence of unity and simplicity. But the system of ordinary knowledge, which the book attempts to communicate with and open up, is very complicated and given to such a diversity of positions that, in order to speak to it and challenge it successfully, you have to try many different approaches and analyses. Don't let this initial level of complexity discourage you. I'm sure that somewhere in *Time, Space, and Knowledge* there is the right access point for each individual reader. Rather than being stopped by something you don't understand, keep looking and trying out different aspects of it until you find your own special 'key'. Once you get a taste of the vision, it will automatically begin to develop further on its own special energy. Until this has happened, it is only necessary to let yourself be accessible to the vision, to approach it with an open mind. I know this is sometimes difficult, because if someone has already made, as part of his or her self-image or lifestyle, an exclusive commitment to one approach to knowledge, such as the empirical, scientific approach, or a traditional meditative approach, then *Time, Space, and Knowledge* might be immediately rejected as violating the logic or methodology of that orientation. This would be a pity, especially since *Time, Space, and Knowledge* does not threaten other approaches to knowledge, and may complement them in interesting ways, if we give it a chance.

In this present anthology, there are many examples of such complementarity, contributed by people of widely varying backgrounds and interests, discussing both theoretical and experiential aspects of their participation in the time-space-knowledge vision. I know that each of these papers required a lot of time and energy to produce, and I'm extremely grateful to their authors for sharing their insights with us. I would also like to thank the staff of Dharma Publishing, as well as David Levin and Steven Tainer, for their part in helping to make these writings publicly available. I am greatly encouraged by the contribution and commitments people have made to this project, and, in turn, I would like to encourage everyone to develop and transmit the time-space-knowledge vision in whatever way or form seems appropriate.

Really? You impose no restrictions on what people make of this vision?

Why should there be restrictions? There's no established tradition. I myself am just a fan of time, space, and
knowledge, supporting them in my own way. Any other
approaches or new ways of developing it are fine as long
as they're not made into a rigid dogma and don't handi-
cap the vision by fitting it back into the models and meth-
odologies of existing ordinary knowledge disciplines. As
long as you really 'go farther' with it, I'm delighted. I
too am thinking of sequels, ways to extend it.

**Will they be at all like the original book, *Time, Space, and
Knowledge*?**

Different content and emphasis will probably dictate
the use of different style and format.

**The first book's style was not as 'sweet' as I might have
expected for such a positive vision. Also, you didn't talk
much about feelings or about coping with the emotional
problems people might have when they first explore the
vision.**

That's all true, and quite deliberate. The job of the first
book was to confront and challenge the aspects of ordinary
knowledge which continually act to obscure or subvert an
appreciation of time, space, and knowledge. Of course, I
also presented the positive aspects of the vision itself
there, but the emphasis was on 'clearing the way'. Also, I
didn't want to promise too much in the way of sweet or
concrete sensations, which would just be objects for the
self-image to grasp at and fasten upon. If you use that kind
of lure to encourage the reader, it's the self-image rather

than 'knowingness' that ends up being encouraged. The enjoyment characteristic of higher 'knowledge' goes far beyond the level of feelings and emotions, which are all still feeding the self-image.

As for your point about coping, I was very concerned that the vision include ways of protecting people from such emotional disturbances, but the protection that I believe to be most effective is the detailed analysis and critique of every feature, position, and presupposition of ordinary knowledge, combined with the natural, effortless, self-liberating quality we were talking about earlier. Neither of these seems very sympathetic to the self, with its problems and its desire to be recognized as someone needing therapy of some kind. But that's exactly why I believe they will provide a better, safer path. The critiques, if they're heeded, will prevent the self from taking up a position within the vision in the first place, so that it does not become overwhelmed or disoriented by the vision's power. If the self does intrude and direct the vision *to* itself, so that it becomes upset somehow, it's still better to analyze the situation carefully with the critical tools I provided, and then allow the instantaneous healing I discussed as being available within each moment to take over.

By the way, as you might expect, given the diversity of positions available within ordinary knowledge, some people have told me that they found the first book *too* sweet and positive. Their experience of the world as being cruel and unjust contradicts the extreme optimism they found characteristic of the book and its vision.

How would you answer such an objection?

I've never denied that time, space, and knowledge can work in very frightening, inhumane ways. All I've done is to point out *why* this might happen, and to emphasize that they also offer us a choice of other directions to go in. I think you can take some of the experiences recorded in this publication to be proof of that.

In the sequels to *Time, Space, and Knowledge* I intend to concentrate on these more positive possibilities. If in the first book or any of its sequels I make a mistake in content, emphasis, or argument, I hope everyone will feel free to contact me and discuss the problem. If, after working within what you've experienced of the vision, and after thinking carefully about the difficulty, you're sure that a change is needed, go ahead and make it. You can then consider the amended version to be the time-space-knowledge vision, and I'll support your decision. I'm sure you'll appreciate how hard it is to produce books of this kind, and will forgive the limitations of my efforts. As I look back on the production of *Time, Space, and Knowledge*, I remember the tremendous difficulties of expressing, organizing, and writing everything so that the vision spoke to us, within the level of ordinary knowledge, while also being protected from possible misunderstandings. It was a lot of work, but I believe it was worth it.

Preface

A great deal has happened since the publication of *Time, Space, and Knowledge* in 1977. There are now 25,000 copies of the book in print, and professors at numerous colleges and universities across the country are using it as a text in their courses. *Time, Space, and Knowledge* workshops have been instituted in thirteen major American cities, and the first nine-month residential training program has been completed at Odiyan, Center for Nyingma Culture, in Northern California. Plans are being made for foreign language translations and for follow-up books exploring further aspects of the vision. In addition, there is the Perspectives on TSK series, of which this is the first publication.

The idea for an anthology was conceived when readers who were asked to share their views on and experiences with *Time, Space, and Knowledge* responded by submitting full-length articles. Further requests brought in additional papers until it seemed more reasonable to consider a series of volumes, with some containing papers on a broad range of topics and others focusing on one, or a few, specific themes.

The present text is divided into four parts. The first contains articles that serve primarily as an orientation for readers who are unfamiliar with the Time-Space-Knowledge vision; however, "Opening Time," by Tarthang Tulku, extends the initial presentation of the vision and includes new exercises as well. Parts Two and Three contain thirteen articles by scholars and professionals who have found connections between *Time, Space, and Knowledge* and their fields of activity—connections which have suggested new ideas, solutions to old problems, and ways of extending or dissolving current boundaries. The last part consists of shorter papers and comments, many of which were written by persons who have participated in one or another of the *Time, Space, and Knowledge* programs mentioned above. In this part, the authors describe, evaluate, or elaborate on transformative experiences associated with their study and practice of the Time-Space-Knowledge vision.

Our sincere thanks go to all the authors for the time and energy they contributed to make this anthology a reality. All of us at Dharma Publishing are grateful for their cooperation, and for their patience during the slow process of getting the publication off the ground.

Like a seed, the Time-Space-Knowledge vision grows naturally, in response to its own inherent dynamism. Still, it needs cultivation to flourish—the digging up of unchallenged assumptions and the intelligent re-vision of ordinary perspectives. The contributions in this anthology exemplify this kind of cultivation in the complementary realms of theory and practice. Consequently, they do not represent work that is merely 'in addition to' *Time, Space, and Knowledge*: they are directly and intimately involved in the development of the vision itself. We hope, and expect, that these writings will prove useful in a variety of ways, and that they will stimulate others to begin their own explorations.

Anyone wishing to submit a paper for possible use in a future publication of the Perspectives on TSK series is encouraged to do so. Analyses, critiques, or applications of *Time, Space, and Knowledge*; statements of personal experience with the vision; and replies to articles in this volume are all welcomed. Manuscripts should be sent to:

Perspectives on TSK
Dharma Publishing
2425 Hillside Avenue
Berkeley, CA 94704

RALPH H. MOON
STEPHEN RANDALL

Introduction

> The capacity of Great Space is never exhausted or compromised by a commitment to one particular trend or world order. Great Space can let anything appear. Great Space supports infinitely many choices of perspective.
> —Tarthang Tulku
> *Time, Space, and Knowledge*

Like Great Space, the Time-Space-Knowledge vision has an unlimited carrying capacity: it freely accommodates familiar points of view, while remaining open to the fresh opportunities that time and space continuously place at our disposal. The variety of perspectives represented in this anthology will not, then, surprise anyone who is already acquainted with *Time, Space, and Knowledge*; instead, the contrasts in its content and approach should serve as further evidence of the radically open intelligence that lies at the heart of this vision.

However, the diversity may come as a surprise to newcomers. To be sure, authors regularly address different subjects and express different opinions, even when writing about the same book, but generally, the range of topics is relatively well confined. Not so in *Dimensions of Thought*.

How, then, can one account for the fact that people with such different backgrounds and interests have been drawn to one work? The answer was hinted at earlier: this delightful variety of opinions and approaches betokens the enormous carrying capacity of the Time-Space-Knowledge vision. The ways in which the vision may be expressed and applied are literally endless.

This gift for accommodation derives, in turn, from the position-free character of *Time, Space, and Knowledge.* The book does not attempt to establish any particular perspective, model, or doctrine; such an effort would only allow it to support programs that shared similar view-points and beliefs. Instead, this vision might be likened to light, which is capable of revealing many different aspects of reality, without needing to change its own nature.

What *Time, Space, and Knowledge* seeks to promote is not a particular vantage point, but a thoroughgoing reexamination of the nature of all appearance, and this, especially at the beginning, involves our becoming aware of how particular 'focal settings' that we have adopted set up and structure appearance, imposing subtle kinds of limitations on what is inherently open and infinite (in a non-mathematical sense of the word). The idea that such structuring can happen is not new; at least since Kant, people have speculated about the extent to which the spectator helps shape what is seen. But for this vision it is not just a matter of our ideas and perceptual apparatus modifying aspects of experience. These 'focal settings' are responsible for *everything in* experience—the appearance of subject, object, perceptual apparatus, ideas—and even the 'appearance' of experience itself. Moreover, *Time, Space, and Knowledge* does not seek to posit this as a new theory, but instead, offers the means for obtaining a firsthand appreciation of the 'fact' and its lived significance.

'Focal settings' are related to points of view or positions. When we observe things in a particular way, from a particular 'position', they take on a characteristic appearance involving concepts, percepts, and much more. Theories, since they account for events *as they appear to us*, end up incorporating these concepts and, ultimately, the particular viewpoint and 'focal setting' on which they depend. Consequently, if the intent is to understand points of view, concepts, percepts, and the like—and this *is* a first step toward the more precise and comprehensive 'knowing' that *Time, Space, and Knowledge* discusses—then the standard approach will not do, in principle. For it involves adopting a particular point of view and then working the associated concepts into a theory: this simply produces an *instance* of the general phenomenon under investigation. That is, any application of the ordinary theoretical approach just produces more data to be understood, and not an understanding of the data.

The fact that *Time, Space, and Knowledge* cannot achieve its purpose and, at the same time, adopt a fixed position, means that there can be no "party line"—and so, as mentioned earlier, no intrinsic limits on the ways in which the vision can be expressed and applied. To put the matter a bit differently, *Time, Space, and Knowledge* is not greatly concerned with *what* we say about the world, *so long as* it is informed by a clear and penetrating 'seeing' that cuts through surface phenomena to what is fundamental in every manifestation.

The book *is*, on the other hand, very concerned with helping to develop that kind of 'vision', a task which, from a particular perspective, seems to first require the breaking of a 'spell' that keeps us from seeing what there is to be seen. The *Time, Space, and Knowledge* exercises help here by allowing for the exploration of a range of experiences that are generally left out of account when we begin our thinking about the realm we inhabit and our place in it. Thus, they provide for a more comprehensive understanding, at the same time as they keep the study of the vision grounded and prevent it from deteriorating into empty conceptualizing. The text plays an equally crucial role: by enabling the readers to locate and challenge the presuppositions involved in our ordinary orientation toward reality, it helps them to incorporate experiential insight gained from practice of the exercises into a broader-based knowing of *all* appearance, standard as well as non-standard.

Together, the reading of the text and the practice of the exercises enable one to experiment with various 'focal settings', so that habitual patterns of thought and experience can be investigated, and their rigid hold loosened. This provides the space necessary for new insights and for the awakening of a latent form of intelligence that is capable of tracking what is ordinarily overlooked. We can then begin to appreciate the opportunities offered by time, space, and knowledge—three fundamental dimensions of appearance which, because they were relegated to the background and largely ignored, were not allowed to show themselves directly. Coming to see all of experience as the dynamic play of these three factors, we also start to recognize that the freedom and fulfillment that have so often seemed lacking in our lives have always been available to us, and have remained 'hidden' only because our manner of searching precluded our finding them.

We realize that a certain pattern of 'minding' kept us systematically distracted from what is of basic importance, while it put forward claims to provide us with all that we needed to, or could, know. But we also see, eventually, that there is no reason to demean or dispense with 'ordinary knowledge', despite this seeming disservice. For 'within' it we find another kind of 'knowingness' which reveals that the 'ordinary' is not really ordinary at all. Having understood the nature of 'ordinary knowledge' more thoroughly, we finally become able to use it to its best advantage, for making our theories more accurate and our lives more satisfying.

Suppose that mankind only used its sense of hearing to collect information about the world. A lot would be missed that could be very important both personally and theoretically. (In particular, nothing would be known about the physical processes involved in being able to hear.) Bringing another sense into play would not require giving up hearing; it would be useful in all the ways it always had been. Actually, that understates the case: the addition of another sense, say vision, would *increase* the usefulness of hearing. And, in terms of understanding, this one added sense would contribute far more than the collection of thousands of extra pieces of auditory data.

The contribution of higher knowledge is something like this: instead of competing with our usual approaches to understanding and fulfillment, it complements and nurtures them. But this analogy should not be taken too literally. What *Time, Space, and Knowledge* wants us to 'see' and explore—namely, time, space, and knowledge—does not require new senses as much as a new sensitivity to what is fully available all the time, although it may be present in an ambiguous form. Another analogy may help make this a bit more clear.

Think about some people from a very isolated culture learning about television sets. On their first encounter, they may take the images to be 'real', believing that there are miniature people and places inside the box; and if there happens to be a violent show on the air, they may be very frightened or upset. Assuming that our imagined people do not know your language and that they would have no idea what you were pointing to if you took the back off the TV set, how would you persuade them that there was nothing to be afraid of? What you want these people to see, the shifting blobs of color on the screen, constitutes the images they are mistaking for realities, and you cannot point at one without pointing at the other as well. They do not need to see something that is not already there; the viewers simply need to shift the focus of their attention so that they may become aware of the nature of what they are seeing.

One thing you might do, of course, is to change channels, not just once, but time after time. Bringing new images onto the screen in fairly rapid succession, and occasionally returning to the original program, may convince these people that there is more (and at the same time, less) going on than meets the eye. If so, they will begin to see for themselves that they have been watching patterns of light rather than people and events. Now this may amount to somewhat of a letdown at first: they may radically shift their opinion and consider the images to be 'unreal'—nothing more than the play of light. But if all goes well, these viewers will, with sufficient familiarity, be able to enjoy watching a television set, and to see either characters involved in dramatic situations, interesting visual images, or both at the same time—without considering any of these perspectives as 'ultimately real'.

The shifting of 'focal settings' that is involved in our study of the Time-Space-Knowledge vision can have somewhat the same effect that the changing of channels did above. Although at the beginning the changes may result only in the appearance of new 'things to see', after a while we may find our habitual focus of attention loosening, and as a consequence, may become able for the first time to see what has been there all along. In the process, certain concepts, 'facts', and principles which had seemed fundamental lose some of their importance as they are seen to be mere reflections of common, but unnecessarily narrow and ultimately rather arbitrary, stances that are adopted moment-by-moment.

Still, this is not the same as finding that these concepts, and the like, are false or mistaken in any absolute sense: they are simply seen in a more incisive way that makes their value and their limitations apparent, so that they may be accepted for what they are without our having to attribute an exclusive truth-value to them. That is, the 'opening' encouraged by *Time, Space, and Knowledge* does not amount to the exchange of one position for another, but amounts, instead, to a 'relaxation' of understanding that allows more possibilities and greater flexibility. So, while it may seem sometimes that *Time, Space, and Knowledge* dissolves certain anchor points of rationality, it is really just a matter of clearing away the underbrush so that more, and not fewer, explorations become possible. Nothing, in the end, is forsaken—although everything may be seen in a new light.

The appearance of new possibilities is not, by the way, simply an occasional, happy result of working with or within the Time-Space-Knowledge vision: such 'openings' are, so to speak, its trademark.

> What is being suggested is not an absolute position describing the truth about a world order, but rather a way of growing without ever falling into a stagnant orientation. Space, Time, and Knowledge are not a fixed set of terms, or a determinate system, but a kind of vehicle to infinite opening. They do not 'mean' something in only a one-dimensional sense; rather, they constantly stimulate us to discover new insights and ways of relating to experience.
>
> Great Space and Time are 'here'. Great Knowledge can

appreciate the opportunities and value they offer. The rest
is just a matter of living out this unfolding vision in everything that we do. This is truly an 'all positive', *life oriented*
path. (p. 215)°

So—and this is an essential point—*there is no fixed goal*
in the study of *Time, Space, and Knowledge.* Understanding the vision is not a matter of seeking and getting
'higher' knowledge which, when obtained, qualifies one as
'certified'. What the vision offers is not a fruit that, as yet,
we are too short to reach up and pluck—even though it
may look that way from one perspective.

> From the point of view of Great Knowledge, there is no
> separation between it and ordinary knowledge; but from
> the view of the latter, there is a separation which must be
> overcome. We therefore feel that we must catapult our-
> selves into a higher condition or 'state'. Such an approach
> is self-limiting; moreover, there is no reason to believe
> that any new 'state-specific' experiences would be gener-
> ally more valid or relevant than our ordinary experience.
> (p. 213)

One must first recognize and then constantly remind
oneself of this open-endedness. This will help counterbal-
ance the inevitable and almost irresistible urge, when first
grappling with the vision, to try to pin it down—to fit it
neatly into one or another familiar scheme. Now, handled
skillfully, this need not create any serious problems. We
may, and perhaps *must*, begin by interpreting *Time, Space,
and Knowledge* in terms of what we already know, just

in order to 'get a handle on' it. But after time, space, and knowledge begin to be appreciated directly, rather than through their various 'agents'—subjects, objects, experiences, and facts—the urge to interpret or locate the vision may diminish. There may come a recognition that the knowledge and fulfillment once sought after are "too 'near' to 'get', and . . . so ever-present that no particular approach is necessary or possible" (p. 305). If so, nothing will have been lost through the initial interpretations, and much will have been gained.

But there is a danger—if interpretation for the sake of establishing temporary 'handholds' gives way to an *identification* of *Time, Space, and Knowledge* with some theory, model, doctrine, or 'path'—of 'freezing' the vision, and thereby losing the unique and useful qualities that it can provide. Such identifications automatically put limits on its powers of accommodation; for if the Time-Space-Knowledge vision is identified with x, then it can only accommodate y if x does, too. Identifications, ignoring the open-ended quality of the vision, also suppress its inherent dynamism. (If you tie a horse to a stake, it will sooner or later reach the end of the tether, no matter how long the tether is; and when the horse does, there is nothing left for it to do but run in circles.)

The greater danger, however, is not to the vision, but to the people who get tangled up in such undertakings. First of all, each such project is bound to fail. To successfully pin down *Time, Space, and Knowledge*'s approach or position, there would have to *be* such an 'approach' or 'position'—and there is neither. A great deal of time could be spent on many unproductive byways, following mistaken expectations. Since people are likely to look at the book in the light of previous identifications, all they will be able to find is the ideas and beliefs that they themselves have planted there. Having found nothing new in *Time, Space, and Knowledge*, they are likely to put it aside, rejecting a potent ally without having given it a chance. For, in a very real sense, they will never have read the book or practiced the exercises, regardless of how many times their eyes passed over the words and how many hours they spent following the instructions.

None of this is to say that people who detect similarities between passages in *Time, Space, and Knowledge* and passages in other works should dismiss them. A careful, thoroughgoing *exploration* of apparent points of connection can be useful in many ways: it may, for example, reveal that the similarities are not simply coincidental. Then, when the reasons for them are seen, people may begin to find other similarities in many unexpected places.

A part of what lies behind this phenomenon is the fact that *Time, Space, and Knowledge* directs our attention to certain extremely fundamental dimensions of *all* appearances: time, space, and knowledge. And these are not *hidden* dimensions: at all times, in all places, and at all levels of knowledge they are not only present, but their 'interplay' *constitutes* everything—every subjective and objective 'thing'—all unified in a way that involves neither parts nor a 'whole', nor even a process. (This should not be taken as a statement about 'reality'; the

Time-Space-Knowledge vision does not involve *any* 'reality'. In fact, "Space, Time, and Knowledge are 'what is' without this meaning that they are things that *are*, such as a fundamental substratum, truth, or reality" (p. 285). Moreover, "freedom, openness, relaxation, power, creativity, intimacy, spontaneity, love, satisfaction and fulfillment—all are first-level representations of the appreciation of Space and Time by Knowledge" (p. 303). So, given the omnipresence and ready 'availability' of space, time, and knowledge, and their intimate connection with fundamental human values, it would seem virtually certain that many aspects of the vision would find expression, in one form or another, in every age and culture.

This, however, does not provide grounds for concluding that any of the doctrines or traditions which preserve these expressions is identical with the Time-Space-Knowledge vision or, for that matter, that it includes any or all previous traditions. This is a consequence of the fact that in one sense, the vision's concerns end where traditions begin: it works directly with the 'layer' of values 'responsible' for the birth and continuation of traditions, philosophies, and even cultures.

An understanding of this last point is especially important for everyone who is seriously involved in a religious tradition. For it means that the Time-Space-Knowledge vision is not something that can collide or compete with spiritual and moral commitments so long as these remain true to their underlying values. The vision, in fact, assures people that everything they hope for, everything of genuine importance, is fully available within their own

tradition. What is necessary, however, is to seek out and
be attentive to the values inherent in the doctrines and
practices being followed; and it is here that *Time, Space,
and Knowledge* can be of assistance. The vision can foster
an opening to the richer elements of any tradition, permitting unlimited growth and transformation from the
inside.

Every religion with a lengthy history has undergone
many changes as it has developed through time and moved
from one place to another. Sometimes these changes dramatically alter certain forms and practices, but if all goes
well, the 'essence' of the religion remains undamaged and
undiluted. In fact, if everything goes really well, these
transformations can bring about even closer contact with
the religious 'heart' of the tradition. From the standpoint
of *Time, Space, and Knowledge*, changes of this latter sort
can be accomplished more often and more readily than is
generally presumed, and they should be encouraged. For
without value-enhancing growth, energy gets diverted
into the maintenance of forms that become rigid ends in
themselves and lose their original human significance.

While talking about religions, one specific case
should probably be considered. Some people have
inferred that Tarthang Tulku's training in Tibetan
Buddhism was crucial in his development of the Time-
Space-Knowledge vision. Others have gone further, seeing *Time, Space, and Knowledge* as presenting a Buddhist
teaching in the language and concepts of Western science and philosophy. Tarthang Tulku, however, does not

believe that his status as a lama gave, or gives, him any special access to the vision. We are all, in his view, equally a part of time, space, and knowledge; no one can own or have special privileges with regard to these precious resources. While he may have opened the door to the vision, everyone, in his estimation, has an equal opportunity to participate in its continual unfolding.

Moreover, even though Tarthang Tulku believes that *Time, Space, and Knowledge* and Buddhism can form a highly compatible and mutually illuminating partnership, he also thinks it is useful to remain aware of the differences between these two, since an identification here can produce the same kinds of problems and obstacles that come with any other identification. Every living religion, including Buddhism, lays varying amounts of stress on one or more of the following elements: rituals, deities, doctrines, symbols, hierarchies, saints, prayers, vows, and devotion. On the other hand, none of these plays a role in *Time, Space, and Knowledge.* Nor, to get a bit more particular, do Enlightenment, meditation, *satori, skandhas, klésas,* yogic disciplines, asceticism, Nirvana, samsara, *kayas, samadhis, siddhis,* and the like. Of course, *Time, Space, and Knowledge* does not suggest that these things are without value. Each aspect of religion in general, and of Buddhism in particular, is or should be connected with the religious 'heart' of the tradition to which it belongs, and *Time, Space, and Knowledge* wants to see that connection strengthened.

Finally, while it has been stressed that *Time, Space, and Knowledge* and the world's religions share important common interests, it is still risky to identify the vision as 'religious', even if one focuses on the 'essence' of religions. It may, for instance, be all right to grant that there is a sense in which the Time-Space-Knowledge and the Buddhist visions are 'one'. But by the time this sense is clearly understood, there may not be anything left to identify with anything else, and until that time, any subtle or explicit belief in their identity, or in some 'ultimate common ground', can only obscure both. The matter can perhaps be summarized as follows: *before* the 'point of understanding', such comparisons are wrong-headed, uninformative, and irrelevant; while *afterwards*, they are right-headed, uninformative, and irrelevant.

The preceding discussion, by taking a position 'outside' of the Time-Space-Knowledge vision and talking 'about' it, has had to remain rather superficial throughout. But its purpose will have been served if it helps you to more fully enjoy the selections in this anthology, and to see them, collectively, as indicative of the democratic nature of the vision—its emphasis on freedom of thought, intelligence, and the opportunity for each person to make his or her unique contribution.

Future volumes of the Perspectives on TSK series will present even more explorations of and connections with the vision including responses to the articles and comments you are about to read. Our sincere hope is that the series, by constantly working toward a broader, more inclusive outlook, and by supporting open and vigorous dialogue, will itself make a contribution to the growth of knowledge, and assist its readers in clarifying and deepening their lived understanding of time and space.

Part One

Ralph H. Moon

A Revolutionary Vision

Tarthang Tulku studied the vast and diversified psychological, philosophical, religious, and scientific traditions of central and east Asia, traditions which had been assimilated and expanded by generations of Buddhist teachers in Tibet. Then, after working for six years with Indian and Western scholars at Sanskrit University in Benares, India, he immigrated to the United States where he founded the Nyingma Institute and established regular contact with Americans and Europeans from all walks of life.

As Tarthang Tulku became more familiar with Western concepts, he "saw the possibility of a visionary medium through which a common ground could be found in the pursuits of knowledge carried out by the various sciences and religions" (p. xxxi).* This vision found expression in *Time, Space, and Knowledge,* and the papers in this volume stand as proof of its ability to bring together persons with a wide variety of interests.

---

*This and all the parenthetical page references that follow are to *Time, Space, and Knowledge.*—Ed.

Although *Time, Space, and Knowledge* was nurtured by and expresses its vision through certain aspects of science, philosophy, psychology, and religion, the vision itself cannot be identified with, nor are its insights limited to, any one or any collection of these fields of study. *Time, Space, and Knowledge* is not an extension or reinterpretation of an already existing body of doctrine, and even though it opens the way for fruitful interaction among disciplines generally considered to be incompatible, it is not a synthesis or melding of them, either.

The desire for such a synthesis is certainly right-minded, as far as it goes, for it is grounded in the recognition that *whatever* reality might be, it cannot consist of separate segments. The regions we isolate and study must, in some way, be thoroughly interacting and interdependent. Yet, the integration of those isolated aspects of reality does not call for assembling pieces we already have; nor does the task call for a 'reduction' of some of the aspects to others. Nothing short of a *new way of seeing* can bring about a precise, informative understanding that comprehends the natural harmony and intimacy of things and, at the same time, preserves and promotes human values. That is what *Time, Space, and Knowledge* offers—the gift of new eyes—a fresh, incisive vision that reveals new insights wherever it may be turned.

Since this book represents a radical departure from tradition, it is difficult to summarize its approach briefly. Still, an analogy with the processes leading up to a scientific revolution can help transmit some of its flavor. In science, problem solving is a way of life, and the existence of unanswered questions is normal and even desirable. In the end, it is the unresolved issues that guide research and, therefore, the extension of scientific knowledge. Moreover, when existing theories and methods prove inadequate, open problems provide the incentive for developing new ideas, tools, and techniques.

Occasionally, however, a logjam occurs. A cluster of related problems refuses to be explained by existing knowledge, and attempts to extend or amend the old theories lead to a proliferation of incompatible ideas and approaches, which only muddies the water further. While, for a time, there appears to be a breakdown in science, the confusion and conflict sometimes signal the start of a period of discovery and transformation. New methodological strategies may be required, however. (The failure of standard problem-solving techniques is, after all, what characterizes this stage of scientific evolution.) A conceptual deadlock of this kind generally calls for new *perspectives* rather than new ideas devised from the old standpoint. So the way is cleared, not by following the ordinary one-at-a-time approach, but by taking a fresh look at the whole collection of problems as symptoms of a deeper difficulty.

The common root of all the problems is often a complex of unconscious assumptions, connected with unnecessarily limited ways of looking at certain fundamental background issues. When these are brought into the foreground, so that the limited perspectives can be challenged and a broader view taken, the old problems frequently vanish and a wealth of new knowledge reveals itself. When this happens, a "scientific revolution" has taken place.

C ertain features of the events just described resemble aspects of the broader human situation. To see this, let us begin, once more, with unsolved problems—not only problems of theory, however, but *the entire range of difficulties* we face in every phase of our personal and collective existence. It is an interesting and possibly suggestive irony that, while our age in many ways exceeds our ancestors' wildest utopian dreams, confusion and trouble remain a persistent fact of life. Indeed, just as happens prior to a scientific revolution, problems seem to be increasing both in number and complexity.

Moreover, our standard strategies are not producing effective, durable solutions. The institutions we have traditionally looked to for guidance—government, business, technology, education, religion, the family—are either facing serious problems of their own, or else finding themselves investing ever-increasing quantities of human energy and material resources on inconclusive research and stopgap programs with unpredictable consequences. In addition, the current proliferation of disciplines and agencies seems to parallel the increase in ideas and approaches during a 'crisis' in the sciences. Here, as there, each one treats only a small part of the larger problem, and frequently these groups work at cross purposes, making the situation even more complicated.

Most people adopt one of three attitudes toward this dilemma. Some attribute these problems to conditions that are beyond our control—population growth, finite resources, human nature, karma, and so on. Others are inclined to blame some person or group of people: government, religion, technology, business, the military, and rock music have all been accused at one time or another, in the belief that eliminating or drastically altering them would cause the problems to ease. Finally, there is the optimistic faith that if we just keep trying, the next technological breakthrough or alternative lifestyle may bring the long-sought relief.

Time, Space, and Knowledge, on the other hand, suggests that there are no grounds for belief in the efficacy of these attitudes. The first amounts to little more than saying that since I cannot see any way to change what needs to be changed, there must not be any such way. Such an inference is fallacious; it is possible that we have been looking in the wrong place. In addition, it encourages resignation, and doing nothing in the face of a bad situation often contributes heavily to its getting worse. The second and third are examples of strategies which have been tried throughout history, without lasting success and without anyone's having stopped to ask whether such solutions might not be implicated in the continuation of problems at all levels—from the most personal and psychological to the most global and concrete.

According to *Time, Space, and Knowledge*, we should consider the possibility that the pile-up of difficulties and confusions, together with the decreasing return on our investment in solutions, indicates the need for a radical change of perspective, and not some new scheme based on old viewpoints. *Time, Space, and Knowledge* claims that these problems, like the ones that plague science prior to a revolution, are generated and perpetuated by narrow and inaccurate assumptions concerning certain fundamental factors in our situation. Because these matters are relegated to the background, their primacy and power remain undetected. What is needed, then, is a shift of focus that brings them into the foreground, where they can be explored in a fresh and penetrating way. The result, *Time, Space, and Knowledge* suggests, will be another sort of revolution, one that is accompanied by vast new understandings and the discovery of untapped and ever-increasing resources.

The factors in question are time, space, and knowledge. These three have, of course, been important to every culture throughout recorded history. The Babylonian world centered around the astrologer-priest, who used his knowledge of the celestial bodies to keep track of and interpret time. More recently, new ideas about the nature and role of space, time, and knowledge have led theoretical physicists and chemists to formulate descriptions of reality as different from classical Newtonian views as the latter are from their Aristotelian antecedents.

Mankind's history of concern and involvement with time, space, and knowledge does not imply, however, that even one of them is well understood. One reason is that standard approaches, including those developed during the past seventy-five years, are methodologically indirect.

Instead of focusing attention on time, space, and knowledge in themselves, they deal only with representatives, or 'agents': objects and locations, experiences and clock-time moments, facts and beliefs.

Now, there is nothing *wrong* with proceeding in this fashion, but it prevents us from seeing the whole picture. For, even though time, space, and knowledge remain continuously 'present' and accessible, the stance we take forces them to appear 'in disguise'. We, in turn, become captivated by the masquerade (indeed, 'we' take the leading role in the ongoing drama) and forget the true identity of the actors. Our appraisal of the situation therefore loses a measure of accuracy. Temporarily 'blinded', we forget that wherever we look, what presents itself to us is space, time, and knowledge—and whatever we do, we are using their resources. Moreover, we view the play of space and time as ultimately serious, and so miss both the light-hearted spirit in which it is offered and innumerable opportunities for fruitful and stimulating participation.

This limiting and deadening ignor-ance of space, time, and knowledge is reversible, however, and realizing the centrality of these factors in the human problems discussed above can provide an incentive to renew our appreciation of them. Throughout history, nations and individuals have battled and haggled over boundaries, and today more than ever we yearn for greater, more open physical and psychological spaces. Life seems to grow more hurried with each passing day, leaving little time to do what is fundamentally important for ourselves and others.

Though we spend our time and energy thinking we are doing something valuable, we seldom achieve any enduring satisfaction. Finally, our time runs out, and there is nothing we can do about it.

Our knowledge, too, has serious limitations. There is never enough information to let us confidently predict the consequences of our actions, and all too often, attempts to solve one problem generate a whole family of new ones. Weapons technology, for instance—knowledge developed for the sake of peace and security—has grown to the point that there is scarcely anywhere in the world that is truly safe. Our industries, using technical know-how to produce goods that lighten our labor and increase our standard of living, have also produced wastes that pollute air, water, and land all over the planet. Even more significantly, however, with all our practical and theoretical knowledge, we still cannot answer, or even accurately frame, questions concerning our world and our destiny—our space and our time—so that we get what we truly want and need, rather than consolations.

Thus, we treat time and space as abstract indices, and knowledge as an epiphenomenon, while looking elsewhere for insight and relief. Alternatives *are* available, however.

> Space and time are not simply backgrounds or supporting mediums for our ordinary pursuits and experience; they can provide a very special and direct form of nourishment for our 'humanity' or human nature, which is usually fed only indirectly through the pursuit of sensory and emotional gratifications. Our attitudes, emotions, and even our actions are usually rather 'closed' states of being. We can

use knowledge to open space and time, and to inspire personal growth and integration. The liberating presence of space and time shows us that within all stagnant and oppressive conditions there is actually room for movement and growth. We do not need to escape from these situations. Knowledge can inspire a new way of being in which the usual difficulties and conflicts which we experience in our daily lives—and which also seem to be inherent in the world situation—can be seen in a new light—they are no longer so rigid or unsolvable. As these experiences take on a more open, transparent quality, we are naturally able to create balance and harmony in our lives, and in our world as well.

When we open all our perspectives and our senses, and learn to view life in a holistic way, we can see that the time, space, and knowledge which have established restrictive perimeters have done so only because they have been insufficiently challenged, explored, and appreciated. We can learn to recognize whatever we experience to be space and time. (pp. xxxviii–xxxix)

There are, of course, limits to the analogy between scientific revolutions and the revolution proposed in *Time, Space, and Knowledge*. The challenging and broadening of perspectives which the latter aims at are not restricted processes culminating in new and 'more accurate' concepts of reality. In fact, major portions of *Time, Space, and Knowledge* are given over to investigating the basis of concepts and the way they ordinarily *interfere* with an appreciation of the openness of Being. The book aims at the penetration of fixed perspectives, boundaries, and divisions until everything is discovered to be 'space', 'time', and 'knowledge'—including the discovery itself.

So, *Time, Space, and Knowledge* does not offer an 'ultimate' scientific theory or philosophical perspective, although it accommodates both philosophy and science. Nor is it a statement of creed for a new brand of spirituality, offering yet another path to a 'more desirable' state of consciousness or existence. Such static goals are incompatible with the open dynamism of its vision.

Instead, the book proposes a continuous, multi-dimensional unfolding—a gentle, balanced, creative explosion. It begins and ends with a fresh appreciation of all appearance, and a new opening to time, space, and knowledge—limitless resources available to us all.

Orientation to TIME, SPACE, AND KNOWLEDGE

The Space-Time-Knowledge vision accommodates the facts of ordinary phenomenal appearance without validating *any* of our presuppositions about them. Activating the vision requires us to recognize and transcend such presuppositions, including those that seem to be embedded in experience—'being *here*, seeing and touching (through the body's sensory capacities) things over *there*', for instance. So, it will be useful to summarize and explore some of our usual orientations, in terms of the vision's three facets.

Space. Look around you. Your eye will most likely fall on one or more of the 'things' in your immediate environment. These 'things' have identities, values, and utilities that offer us one range of possibilities, while excluding others.

This article was originally distributed in mimeographed form at a lecture given by Tarthang Tulku shortly after the publication of *Time, Space, and Knowledge*; much of the article was extracted from that book.—Ed.

But notice that, just as valleys are the constant companions of mountains, wherever there are 'things', there is always a distance separating them. If you shift your normal perceptual focus, from objects to the space or room between and around them, you will find that this space itself has properties that contrast in interesting ways with those of the 'things' it 'houses'. For example, it seems to be impossible to distinguish one region of space from another, except in terms of the things that occupy them or lie in their vicinity. All space, then, seems to be of one 'flavor', whereas objects come in all varieties. Furthermore, space does not seem to be exclusive in the way that 'things' are. The same space that is now the scene of one 'happening' has accommodated many others in the past, and will continue to do so in the future.

After 'studying' space for a while, you may get the sense that it is far more important than we ordinarily consider it to be. It is space that permits movement; in fact, without space, there could be no 'happenings' at all, and for that matter, no 'things'. And yet, we have no trouble imagining space without 'things' and events. So space appears to be somehow fundamental. What is more, the longer we look for space, the more we find. It seems to be *virtually* omnipresent.

The exceptions to the presence of space, of course, are the objects that occupy portions of it. Objects give the appearance of being solidly 'walled off' from the space that surrounds them. But according to science, they consist of atoms, with vast spaces around and within them. So, in theory at any rate, seemingly solid objects, too, turn out to be primarily space.

In order to experience this insight more vividly, imagine some object (a human body, for example) and enlarge it until it is of gigantic proportions. As you examine it, allow yourself to move closer and closer until you approach the first boundary. Now let the object become larger still, and when you locate the spaces or gaps in the boundary, move inside. Continue your exploration until you run into another barrier. Again, let it become larger and larger until you can move through it as well. Continuing in this way you can penetrate down to, and through, the subatomic level. If you then 'look back' at the object that originally presented itself as opaque and dense, all you will find is space. Even the features and surfaces you encountered along the way turn out to be space—transparent, shining outlines that offer no resistance either to your gaze or to your passage.

Seeing 'things' as being undifferentiated space is a first step toward grasping the 'space' dimension of experienced *situations*. A specific situation has a forcing quality: by finding ourselves 'in' one, we also find that certain responses are incumbent upon us, while others are desirable, and many more are impossible. We can think of this as a matter of what that 'space' offers and excludes. But by opening up the partitions of that space—starting with the presented objects, and later working with the entire interrelated complex that constitutes the situation—we learn that other possibilities are also present or 'accessible' in some way.

If the process of opening is carried far enough, it may become apparent that infinite possibilities are already 'here', and that space is more a field of opportunities than one of positions and locations. It is then appropriate to refer to this unbounded openness as *Great Space*. And since the situation with which we began *is* Great Space (without the latter's being anything), such a situation is the present bearer of *all* of Great Space's possibilities. The limitations that were the starting point of the process of expansion can no longer be found!

The Great Space dimension of 'ordinary' situations is always fully 'present' and 'available', but usually it is arbitrarily obscured so that we can build little demarcated nests that allow us to avoid being overwhelmed by an infinity of possibilities. Our comfortable little field can be called *lower space*. It is made to order for the ego, but it is also frustrating, because too much inflexibility has gone into its construction, and too much spontaneity and openness has been shut out. We starve ourselves in order to survive as 'selves'.

Time. Should anyone ask us what time is, we might be hard put for an answer. It seems clear that time serves to locate us in a past-present-future structure, but even that becomes a bit puzzling when looked at more closely. The past is no longer, the future is not yet, and the present is gone before it has a chance to be established. Yet, despite its apparent insubstantiality, time seems to relentlessly move on, carrying us with it. As it brings new things into being, it simultaneously tears down what had been built up before. This tripartite, linear time, then, carries the consequences of transitoriness with it as a necessary feature.

There is, however, a 'fourth time', *Great Time*, that is vital and expressive. It is the dynamism made possible by the complete openness of Great Space, which allows everything and inhibits nothing. Great Time is potentiated by Space and, in turn, expresses Space in an infinity of manifestations.

Ordinarily, time is used in a much more exclusive way—as an index or locating device for expressing the fact that certain 'things' *exist*, thereby excluding other things from being. Like the openness of Space, the dynamism of Time is threatening to us. In its evocation of Space, there is the constant danger of its sweeping away or penetrating our claims to exclusivity and discreteness.

Starting with our ordinary view, with its emphasis on objects and causes and effects *in* time, it is impossible to see that all delineations, differences, significations, and events (constituting us and our realm) *are* a narrow sampling of the play of Great Time. So we need, at least at the beginning, to change our orientation somewhat. Instead of seeing yourself as doing something *in* time, try seeing 'your doing something in time' as itself a manifestation of 'time'. For example, consider that your earlier expansion of the object, and your discovery of vast, open spaces, were, in fact, the work of 'time'.

Knowledge. Ordinary knowledge involves 'facts' about 'things'. It is something *we have*: the subject knows, and the object pole is known. But if we can learn to see situations rather than '*things*', and situations as not being defined by their 'things'; if we can come to recognize 'content' as being a limitation on 'space' drawn up by 'time', then there will also be a new kind of 'knowledge' in this apprehension.

Knowledge is the goal or the fruit of this vision—a fruit that is itself beyond the concern for 'getting', approaching, or defining. Rather than being merely its specified end point, this goal is actually the *basis* of the path to understanding.

Great Knowledge is the immediate and knowing dimension of all reality and experience. It is the interplay between the openness of Space and the expressive creativity of Time. Great Knowledge is not something which knows something; it is simply the presence of reality as 'knowingness'.

At the same time, Great Knowledge keeps fully abreast of the interplay of Great Space and Great Time. By using more knowledge, we can appreciate more of the presence of 'space' and 'time'. In doing so, we will be able to open up 'space' and 'time' to Great Space and Great Time without being overwhelmed, because instead of trying to maintain a very narrow view in the face of these infinite dimensions, we can have Great Knowledge as our base. However, this is only possible if we can give up the aggressive stance of *our* being the knower. We must open to the 'knowing' that is given with all appearance, borne along with its 'space' and 'time' aspects.

Reevaluating our ordinary understandings of time, space, and knowledge and considering new perspectives on them helps to counteract the tendencies that ordinarily keep us from contacting the infinite dimensions that are available to us. Being habitually 'out of touch', we do not flow—float—properly. Our senses, ideas, and physical capacities are blocked in some ways. A lower order structuring space sets up these problems, but does not allow us the capacity of penetrating the nature of our lower space and of its relation to Great Space. We simply do not know that the opaque surfaces which define discrete things—and the frustrating mental and physical blocks and limitations we experience—are essentially related. Both kinds of 'walls' are 'space'—a lower space that can be opened up to Great Space. Even the gulf separating subject and object can be transcended. If we can reach a higher and more open space, all difficulties can be dissolved.

Our perceptions of various spaces and 'things' reflect different levels and types of analysis. For any given level of analysis, there is the appearance of 'objects' only because a very precise 'focal setting' or perspective is maintained. The basic, absolute, or opaque character that some things have for us is due to our unwillingness to change this point of view, or to our assumption that it cannot be done.

What we perceive as solid or opaque 'things', produced by a given 'setting', defines by contrast what we perceive as the 'space' of that level. So, by attending *only* to the apparently solid things and the contrasting space resulting from one particular 'setting', we cannot discover the actual nature of either 'existence' or appearance.

Throughout history, we have been maintaining a fixed and limiting 'focal setting' without even being aware of doing so. Yet, although our familiar world seems to depend upon this 'setting', if we become able to change the 'setting', fantastic new knowledge and appreciation of life can emerge.

The idea of discovering new spaces may seem at first to be a purely abstract, intellectual endeavor, but in fact it is rooted in the deeply felt need to find an alternative to the sense of restriction and confinement which each of us experiences in our daily lives. This feeling of lack of space, whether on a personal, psychological level or an interpersonal, sociological level, has led to the experience of confusion, conflict, imbalance, and general negativity within modern society. We find ourselves setting up strict definitions of territorial boundaries, either as individuals or as larger groups or nations—and great amounts of our energies are utilized in protecting and defending these boundaries.

But if we can allow our perspectives and presuppositions to be 'opened', our experience will change. The anxiety and frustration which result from our sense of limitation will automatically be lessened, and we can increase our ability to relate sensitively and effectively to ourselves, to others, and to our environment.

By employing new 'focal settings' and seeing the way they work, we can come to *an overall understanding which is itself a kind of space,* and which explains, expresses, and *is* everything. Though it may seem to go against our ordinary world-view, an understanding—or *vision*—can itself be the revealing basis of all reality. And even an attention to our ordinary space may help to expose a comprehensive vision based on what we have called Great Space.

It is this that gives value to the exercises and explorations suggested so far. This approach does not use the associations characteristic of ordinary perceived space to trick us into accepting an unusual, but still 'lower space' theory regarding 'the identity of space and objects'. Rather, it uses the perception of 'spaciousness' in a healthy working relationship with that of physical and mental objects to break up the frozen condition of our 'lower space' and thereby allow an understanding of Great Space to be present. The exercises and discussion constitute an investigation aimed at supplementing ordinary 'knowing' —which is something that 'we' have—with Great Knowledge, which cannot be appropriated by a 'self' and does not endorse lower level theories of any sort.

Each stage of practice consists of an opening up or dissolving of a limiting focal setting on the infinity of Great Space. Each stage involves a relaxation of our hold on progressively more fundamental facets of the output of a particular setting. We might say that there is a reciprocal dynamic connection between the focal setting and its output. This relationship allows us to change the setting by relaxing our insistence on perpetuating its effects.

If conducted properly, this type of engagement can result in the attainment of a new kind of 'focal setting' —one which is not just a macro- or micro-adjustment within a particular space, but which actually opens up qualitatively new 'spaces' wherein ordinary awareness and its clumsy conceptual structures are inoperative.

Eventually, we can discover a space that involves no concepts at all, since concepts are simply indications of the relative opacity and resistance of a particular space.

Thoughts, concepts, and distinctions are the product of a 'space' which could be considered similar to an enclosing chamber that filters and inhibits input from the 'outside' —casting shadows and causing echoes or impingements, bombardments, and fragmentations to occur within its walls. Space should accommodate, be open to, and make room for things. But in our ordinary space, 'making room' has become 'making a room'—lower space is like a walled enclosure.

If we can render these walls transparent without thereby setting up new walls and points of view, the notion of inside and outside is thus deactivated, and the experience of internal collisions and interactions ceases. This is then something like Great Space. It may seem to be a condition extremely different from our usual one, but such a distinction and comparison is only perceived from within the limited point of view of lower space, and does not apply in the more open and accommodating perspective. This does not suggest that Great Space, unlike lower spaces, has no concepts and distinctions operative 'within' it. Great Space is not a particular condition, characterized by certain things being present or absent. There are no concepts, and, there is also no 'Great Space which is distinguished by an absence of concepts.' Great Space is not a 'thing' and is not different from our lower space.

The accommodating quality—represented at its peak by Great Space—is complete at precisely the point where the notion of a space, which to a greater or lesser degree allows or accommodates a 'thing', collapses. The openness and allowing are greatest when not filtered through a 'thing which allows'.

The opening process discussed here is actually conducted by 'time'. For it to proceed smoothly, without unnecessary detours, we must learn to work directly with 'time', and to see why it 'goes'. This, in turn, requires relating the 'present moment', which our lower 'knowing' reveals, to the higher dimension we have called Great Time. To facilitate the needed understanding, let us next consider a few exercises that can move us in the direction of recognizing the structure of appearance as being 'time' and 'knowledge'. After that, to close this presentation, we shall take a brief look at the path from ordinary to Great Time.

Contemplating Lower Time

Since we consider ourselves to be separate objects *in* time, continuous in a changing world, we try to hold the 'self' and other familiar objects down, treating them as being relatively stable and fixed. This leads us to ignore much of the expressive and transforming character of time, and as a result, we cannot face up to change. We are often sluggish and stuck in ruts; we are not fluid, amenable to constructive transformation. Our power to mold and change our environment is similarly restricted. Instead of opening directly to the possibilities offered by higher time, we can only try to learn and take advantage of the lawlike regularities that reflect the structure of our variant of lower time.

This 'lower time' is a condition that is in force when the 'self' is set up as an independent entity located in time, surrounded by a spatial environment, and seeing objects separated from it by an intervening distance. The 'self', in turn, is an impoverished version of the 'present', a fact that manifests itself in the inherent *directedness* of the 'self's' position. The 'self' is always up to something, going somewhere, intending something. This amounts to a reflection of the tripartite structure of 'lower time', with its present always coming from somewhere and then moving on.

To be in this kind of present is to be continually off balance and frustrated. 'Things' are here, in the present, only to pass out of reach. 'Things' are desired (due perhaps to previous such losses in the past) but are 'not yet'. We have become so conditioned by this trend that all our hopes and aspirations amount to filling up little slots in a sort of personalized past-present-future grid. *We are literally timing ourselves away.*

The 'time' functioning in our space can cause tremendous damage and suffering if we refuse to see its real message, for we are then at its mercy, and are borne along by it at a feverish pace. Lived time goes too quickly; we never have enough of it. For this reason, fulfillment is hard to obtain. But the issue is not whether clock-time in this realm is faster or slower than in some larger space. It is that we have little capacity for opening to the infinity that 'time' really offers and communicates. We do not *let* satisfaction be a reality; we try to *achieve* it in the future, to capture it and tie it down, making it a 'present'. Under such circumstances, we experience great tension and pressure.

Seeing that our experience brings us suffering can serve as a message, informing us of an error that must be corrected. Or perhaps there really is no error, and these 'misfortunes' themselves can be apprehended differently. But we cannot yet see or do this, except as a fantasy. So we need to listen to the message brought by 'time', as much as we can open to it.

Note the *feeling* you have of the 'future', and then do the same for the 'past'. Explore each of these carefully: notice how these elements crop up in your thinking, locating your present experience and putting it in a broader context. Eventually, you may see that each 'present moment' of experience has a trifurcated structure, and when you do, attend to this closely. Now you might think that this is not working with the real past and future, but only with our thoughts about them—and that is true. But it is precisely this polarization of experience, and this intentional, directed, urgent quality, that gives rise to the flow of lower time and the emergence of 'real' subsequent moments. So it is very valuable to learn as much as you can about this aspect of lower time.

Once more, notice the past-present-future configuration of the situation you are currently experiencing, and select one pole—the future, perhaps. Now move your sense of located and embodied identity 'into' that felt pole. Look quickly! There is another moment, and 'you' are 'outside' again, located in a new past-present-future formation. Then take *that* 'you' and put it into *that* future pole. Again, another 'you' will emerge into a third past-present-future.

Just keep doing this, always going into one of the three poles of the experience you find yourself 'in'. After much practice of this kind, a 'knowledge' that is not 'yours', but is borne along with all 'time', will show more of what is

involved in the surfacing of the 'self' in each situation—
how its locatedness and its alleged independence from the
manifesting quality of 'time' arises. Notice, too, the special
'charge' that the 'self'-component of each of these situations has as the *doer*. The 'self' feels like an agent, domi-
nating its passive surroundings. Pay attention to this on a
moment-by moment basis, and consider that when the self
'comes out', it has not thereby really become other than a
facet of what 'time' is bringing. Also contemplate the
possibility that even when the 'self' seems most clearly to
be doing something—when it is thrusting itself 'back' into
one pole of ordinary time—every part of its effort may be a
narrowing of 'time', or a narrow presenting of 'time'. We
are 'time', even when we feel separate from it.

This exercise can prove to be very helpful in facili-
tating what we generally term personal growth, although that is not its sole or ultimate intent. The inertia
we generally experience, our resistance to change, derives
from the fact that the 'self' we try to improve is simply a
summary or generalization of many instantaneous presentations of 'time'. (Actually, this is only how it seems from
the perspective of trying to reestablish a proper relation
with Great Time: other points of view are possible. However, this one suffices for our present purpose.) It is much
easier to initiate change and improvement if we work
with the 'self' emerging from 'time', when it is just getting
set up.

Sooner or later, however, it is necessary to challenge
the notion that the 'self' ever 'comes out' of 'time'. So,
when you have become proficient with the exercise in the

form described above, try reversing the self as being the 'knower'. Consider, instead, that your environs, and all the 'things' in it, have a 'knowing' aspect and are 'knowing' *you!* (This subject-object reversal may also be treated as a separate exercise, and can be practiced in a wide variety of different circumstances.)

So far, the conduct of this exercise probably 'takes time' on the same standard time scale as any other activity. We might represent time as a series of finite points:

A ·   B ·   C ·   D ·   E ·   F ·

In finding futures within futures within futures, and so on, we are not really finding more of what was in—or available through—the first (trifurcated) point of the exercise. Rather, we are just going from point to point of clock time, while working with *thoughts* of 'the future'. But gradually, as we get used to the idea that we *are* 'time', and as more knowledge comes into play (tracking more of the 'time' that is available), the situation changes. Our capacity for opening to experience and energy may greatly increase. So, while another person standing next to us may only be able to enjoy tiny packets of experience in a point-by-point manner, our experience could be represented in the following zigzag diagram:

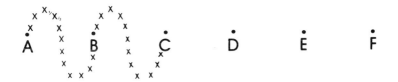

That is, we can have many experiences, *apparently* between two directly linked points (A and B). At first it might seem that we are stretching the time of point A, drawing it out like a strip of rubber. But actually, from the perspective of Great Time, *there are no points.* As an approximation to this higher level statement, we can use zigzags to diagram a situation where one person sees a point of a certain magnitude, while we see more. This 'more' will perhaps still take on the character of a series of points, arranged in a zigzag formation and possessed of a past-present-future structure. We can track what our friend sees (A and B) without accepting these points as 'all there is', or even as solid points. And we (or 'knowingness') can also enjoy the time indicated by the x's.

However, we can do even more. For, as we travel along from x to x, we may remember how 'we' are given as being located in a point. We are 'time' and can embrace more of it (even if we have to do so by forcing it into a zigzag-series character), rather than holding aloof from it, skimming along on the top. Thus, 'between' any two of the x's, we may again get:

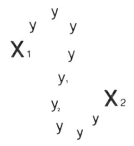

This also need not involve accepting the x's as solid points. Now, between any two of these y's we could get another ordered stream of experience in the same way (along with the experiences of the x's, y's, and the A, B, C, etc.).

$$Y_1 \quad z \quad z$$
$$z$$
$$z$$
$$z \quad z \quad z \quad z$$
$$z$$
$$z$$
$$z \quad z \quad Y_2$$

And between any two points in *that* stream, we could . . . Meanwhile, our friend is stuck on A, B, C, D, and so on.

But there is a catch here. It appears at first that there is a standard time line, and then a series of nonstandard departures from it. This framework breaks down at a certain point, however. In the midst of our exploration of *new* time lines, we may come upon what looks like *the original, standard one* (points A, B, C, D). All the usual, familiar things are there.

But this does not mean we have 'surfaced' or returned to *the* ordinary time. Basically, what eventually emerges from such encounters is the insight that there is not *a* surface, *a* time line that is *actual*, or one that 'we' are on exclusively. This means not just that there might be many such lines, but that the notion of discrete 'lines' is itself wrong.

All this is just a way of winning back to the infinity of Great Time, which does not itself involve a 'going' or diffusion. So, as you open more to 'time' and 'knowledge', you will stop generating these wavelike series of points (all of which are narrowings) and, instead, enjoy a new type of experience, a kind of smooth continuum, which could be represented like this:

which becomes

_____

This, in turn, becomes

.

—not a point in a series, but a centered abiding which in turn becomes a centerless center. This centerless center, which is not enervated by any 'going', may then be seen to be 'everywhere'.

The Path from Ordinary to Great Time

Time, Level One. This involves the ordinary sense of time as a rather abstract index for states and events while also carrying the existential character of being an inescapable and compelling force. We can characterize the whole state of existence in which we find ourselves as being due to 'lower time', although this 'time' cannot yet be detected directly.

'Lower time' is the particular version of Great Time which a specific focal setting on the openness of Great

Space allows, and amounts to an attempted taming and appropriation of Great Time for egoistic purposes. We have borrowed from Time all our energy and capacity for measuring, predicting, discovering, controlling, and communicating. These activities are all distorted versions of Great Time's intimacy with Great Space and its evocation of Space's vastness. But we have allowed ourselves such limited access to Time's dynamism that our little structures are continually blown away. Great Time exhibits something—thus showing the openness of Great Space which permits 'being' and 'happening'—and then breaks it down to exhibit something further. This series (of what from one point of view are misfirings) is the only pattern we know. In fact, this pattern is what we *are*, so we 'go along with it' even if it can sometimes seem quite threatening.

The pattern, however, is not a necessary condition, or even one that is ultimately true. But given our 'knowing', it is the only way 'lower time' can express the infinity that is 'here', since what we can perceive of it—moments—are small and 'cannot hold much at a time'.

Such 'time' not only arranges our 'passage' but structures it in terms of specific encounters. Usually, we become so caught up by this continual stream of particular encounters and times that they prevent us from really getting on with what is most essential. This potentially endless diffusion is the 'lower'—rather distorted—version of Great Time's infinite expression of Great Space, and makes a very effective trap or maze when not properly understood. 'Time' times out our ordinary experience—of starting points, travels, and destinations—but it does so by presenting what could amount to an infinitely variable number of encounters within a completely timeless 'interval' (timeless in the sense of conventional time).

In one way or another we tend to ignore Great Time and thus are led along by it, rather than enjoying or learning from it. We get stuck in a certain track, structured in terms of one set of meanings or another, and we are then forced to observe the ramifications of that track. In fact, the very logic operative within our realm reflects the structure of our 'lower' time. Logical problems and paradoxes can be considered as a sign that such a 'lower time' structure is in force, and that there is another perspective which should be considered. Deeply thinking things through may be the first step toward approximating higher time, and is the point of the *penetrating* investigations suggested at the start of our discussion.

Time, Stage Two. Though deep thinking and an intellectual transcendence of isolated 'things' can initially be helpful in opening our perspective, at a certain point this may simply amount to trading one set of meanings for another more subtle one. To be free of this whole dependence on meanings and the type of time that they involve, it is necessary to develop more insight, new 'knowing' capacities—otherwise thinking, and even 'penetrating', just go on indefinitely. Essentially, what is needed is a more experiential acquaintance with 'time'.

Whereas the first stage of relating to time is devoid of any direct experience of the 'lower time' which it is said to involve, the second stage consists of a wide range of experiences with 'time', some of which have already been suggested in the discussion of the exercises in the preceding section. It turns out that the problems presented by 'lower time' are precisely due to our ignoring 'time', whereas even a slightly intimate glimpse of it may show that 'time' is not at all oppressive. Time, any 'time', is actually *enabling*, not *restraining*, if appreciated and used with the right 'knowledge'.

Initially, second-stage experiences of 'time' may show it to be like a 'flow' or a flashing, dynamic factor. This happens because ordinary knowing makes it conform to our familiar serial progression of events and our sense that there are things that must somehow have been created or brought into being. If we cling to 'self' and 'thing' presuppositions in the face of a glimpse of 'time' as flowing or flashing, it may seem like an autonomous force 'doing' us or pushing us around. But very soon we may realize that we are only imagining victims where there are none— there is only 'time'.

'We' can learn to allow brief 'knowings' which track more of 'time' and which are broad and impartial enough to take into account our 'self', observed objects, and other background items, all as being given with 'time'. It therefore becomes possible for such a 'knowing' to 'tap' the dynamism of 'time'. To the extent that the result of such a momentary insight is again assimilated to the concerns and interpretations of the ego, we can enjoy more mental energy and more physical power as well. This seems like a veritable control of the direction of ordinary time.

Though this emphasis on 'control' falls far short of real insight, it sums up the observed fact that "things are getting better," that "things are going more my way." To understand such trends, consider that the apparent serial order of ordinary time "going my way" can at this stage be seen to derive from the flow or flashing of 'time'—it is *a tame summary* of 'time'. In the same way, on the ordinary level, 'objects', persons, and continuous identities generally are seen to be convenient summaries of time sequences. The flow of ordinary time is therefore fulfilling or satisfactory just to the extent that the undiminishable freedom and variety offered by Great Space and the unconquerable vitality of Great Time are preserved in the *perceived* outputs of 'time'. It is a matter of how much a higher 'knowing', in its enjoyment of the play of Space and Time, is left unobscured. 'Control' is therefore just the *self's* way of describing the result of opening to a greater appreciation of 'time'.

Meditation can be much more precisely oriented at this stage, and may progress quickly, since it is grounded in greater confidence and expansiveness, due to the deep sense that no state of affairs is irrevocably 'bad', or a 'trap'. We can also learn to appreciate the immediate presence of both 'knowing subject' and 'known objects' without clinging to the view of them *as* those things. We can see them as presentations, with ourselves as part of each presentation. It is then possible for previously hidden dynamics to show themselves within and as the situation; each concrete presentation is seen as an appreciative embodiment of an active 'presenting'. Thus, each is recognized to be a kind of *knowledge,* a stalwart witness-bearer to 'time's' presenting character. 'Time's' dynamism may then be appreciated as expressing the open accommodation of Great Space. More precisely, *the presentation is itself* the appreciation of 'time' as allowed by Space and as, in turn, expressing Space. No additional act of appreciation is necessary.

Time, Stage Three. This is Great Time, the universal bearer which does not do, bear, or express 'things'. Great Time is not a thing or a process and is not disposed in one way rather than in another. It is not conditioned by anything nor does it condition anything. There 'is' nothing, and this is not meant as a statement about some objective, absolute truth of 'the way things are'. Great Time is neither lawlike nor random; it is not a happening or a 'taking place' at all.

The clinging to a reality, a cosmic truth or principle—something that 'is' and is 'out there' to be realized, grasped, or reconciled with—is not relevant to the Great Time vision. Great Time is not a setup or a mysterious force: we might say that it is the inseparable partner of Great Space, the other member of the primordial marriage and love affair. The unrestrained fulfillment of the interplay of Great Space and Great Time is an intimacy that is complete and *uncontrived.*

This intimacy involves neither 'things' nor a subsuming field, just Great Space and Great Time. It is the shattering—and yet natural—surfacing of our real *Being.* This intimacy applies to us; it is not elsewhere, beyond the turmoil and isolation of the ordinary world. It is 'here', the only difference being that a Great Space and Great Time view is taken rather than a 'self' and 'thing' view.

When fully appreciated, Great Time is seen to be a kind of perfectly liquid, lubricious dimension: it is quintessentially 'slippery'. For this reason—although there seem to be movement and separate places to move to on the first level, and still more open, fluid possibilities of movement on the second level—on the third level there is no 'going', and there are no separate places. It is as though all the friction in the world were removed—nothing can then walk away from anything else. So, from a third level view, an eternity of 'straying' still leaves us very much 'at home', intimately united.

Tarthang Tulku

Opening Time

I

What is five minutes like? How much experience can it encompass? How much can be accomplished and how much fulfillment found in a five-minute interval? It is common knowledge that the same amount of clock time can seem longer or shorter, depending on whether it involves painful or pleasurable experiences, and on the overall context. But in exploring the Space-Time-Knowledge vision, we can discover that time is variable in still another way, one quite unlike this subjective variation in judging the duration of a standard clock-time interval. This discovery involves using more 'knowingness', and thereby supercedes the distinction between the variable/subjective and the fixed/objective. It amounts to contacting more of the 'space' and 'time' that are available in each apparently fixed and limited interval of ordinary time.

As a preparation for this, it would be helpful to review some material in *Time, Space, and Knowledge*: the exercises in Part One, exercise 16 ("Space-Time-Knowledge on the Conventional Level"), the discussion in chapters 7 and 8 on the self's tendency to draw apart from 'time', the "zigzag diagram" (pp. 178–84), and exercise 30 ("A Subject-Object Reversal").* All of these will serve to stimulate a 'knowingness' that sees us *as* 'time' and appreciates 'time' more fully, recognizing that it has no intrinsic limits.

At first, because of the tendency to fit it into our ordinary view, the greater appreciation of 'time' this knowledge brings will be rendered as the enjoyment of quantitatively more time, supporting more experiences. This is still only a second-level view of 'time', but it nevertheless represents an opening that can and should be explored further. Therefore, the following exercise is offered.

Set a timer to ring after five minutes has elapsed. Sit quietly, remaining as aware and awake as possible, and see 'how much' experience you can have during this timed period. Several different approaches are possible in this regard. You might want to work with thoughts, sensings, and experiences, keeping track of the approximate number of them that can be accommodated within five minutes. You could, for instance, use a string with a series of knots in it to mark the passage of each thought, counting up the total only when the session is over. Or, on a more subtle level, you could work with awarenesses or 'knowings' that are attuned to a more open-ended *pres-*

---

*Readers who do not have a copy of *Time, Space, and Knowledge* readily available are encouraged to study "A Revolutionary Vision" in this volume.

ence and are not so content-oriented (they are not aware-nesses *of* things). Again, try to maintain an estimate of the number of these entertained in five minutes.

You should find plenty of things to count, although it may be hard at times to know where one 'item' leaves off and the next begins. You need not worry about this, how-ever, since a rough approximation is sufficient here, and it *is* difficult to individuate 'things' of this kind consistently and without being arbitrary. On the other hand, it can happen that, while practicing the exercise, you open up so much that the ordinary chatter of events comes to a halt. If you find yourself with nothing to count, first make sure that you are really *open*—transparent, in a way—rather than merely sleepy (too loose) or too tight (from being engaged in the ongoing reinforcement of an allegedly open position). If one of the latter is the case, there are actually *many* things happening that can be counted if you look sensitively.

If you *are* open, in a higher knowledge way that is not currently picking up lots of countable traces, just abandon the counting exercise for a while, and deepen and expand this other kind of experience. Here, as with the other *Time, Space, and Knowledge* exercises, it is important to remain flexible, that is, ready and willing to incorporate whatever presents itself into your practice.

After tasting this quiet, open space for a time, see if you can 'steer' this openness back into a more playful experiential sequence that can be enumerated. Just as we accommodated the openness, so it, in turn, should be amenable to 'happenings', without this involving a deterioration in the level of practice. It is possible to simultaneously apprehend the countable events *and* appreciate their 'open, unoriginated status'. In fact, this is what allows us to increase our totals in the versions of the exercise that follow.

After doing this exercise on a number of occasions, the totals from the various sessions may approach a fairly consistent figure: You can then use this number as the standard for the next series of practice sessions. In these sessions, conduct the same test of your capacity for utilizing time, but limit each session to four minutes. See if, with sufficient practice, you can register the same total that you had in the final round of five-minute periods. When you can, use this same score as your goal for three-minute sessions. Continue in this way until you can enjoy what had previously been a typical five minutes' worth of experience in a one-minute session.

Perhaps the simplest illustration of how this might work is a strictly mathematical one. Initially, five minutes might seem like an atomic or fundamental 'unit time'—the smallest period you notice as constituting a 'change in time'—particularly when you are caught up in ordinary, outward-oriented actions. However, this unit interval can be divided into five one-minute intervals, and it requires only a little more attention to become aware of the 'passing' of each of these individually. So one minute can, under these circumstances, replace five minutes as our basic unit of experienced time. Then each minute, in turn, can be further subdivided into sixty seconds, each of which is observable so long as we maintain a relaxed, but concentrated state of awareness. The minimum significant unit of

time is now but one three-hundredth of what it was originally, and yet we may find that we are able to use each of
these one-second intervals for thoughts, sensings, and so
on, just as we previously used five minutes.

This way of exemplifying the emergence of more
'knowing' of 'time' is useful, but is not entirely faithful to
the process. For, the noting of smaller and smaller mathematical divisions requires that our individual 'aware-
nesses' become temporally shorter and shorter. Moreover,
the quantitative *total* of time that we are aware of would
remain fixed, regardless of how many tiny discrete intervals we might register. Neither of these limitations
applies to the case of using more 'knowingness' to track
'time'. And finally, even though an awareness restricted to one-second intervals would allow us to go back to
the period of time we began with and enjoy three hun-
dred such points, the important consequence of this exercise is not that we can develop a new skill and then use
it to have even more experiences in subsequent five-minute intervals. It is, instead, that the boundaries distin-
guishing five minutes from one second are unreal in a
certain sense, and so *any* amount of experience constituting five minutes could also be had in one second.

The 'small' interval is not really smaller, nor is the
'larger' one really larger. For as we will see in a later
section, the more extensive duration and unfolding movement of time required to constitute an apparently longer
interval can be discovered to be illusory. So we may indeed
suspect that such quantities are only relative and not intrinsic to time. For these several reasons, then, when we

are learning to cultivate more 'knowingness' of 'time', the mathematical analogy for expanding a certain interval should not be taken literally. We will, however, find an important use for this mathematical process of division in section III.

To emphasize the insight that smaller and larger intervals are inherently the same, try working with a five-second practice session. Learn to use this length of time with increasing effectiveness, marking your progress as before. It may eventually be possible for you to enjoy the same amount of experience as in the case of five minutes. Where then is the real difference between these intervals? What is the sense of such distinctions, except to characterize the capacity of our typical, but arbitrary, approach to knowing time?

II

Although deep experiential acquaintance with 'time' is not limited to a first-level series of tiny, quantified temporal fractions of some larger total, the ability to be sensitive to such units does follow as an indirect consequence of the more second-level 'knowing'. Moreover, this ability is particularly valuable when one is visited by strong emotions and moods. In the next phase of practice, then, you will carry your newly acquired capacity for knowing time into the experiences of daily life.

Investigate the tiny time intervals constituting an experience of pain or anger lasting for five minutes or so. What is the overall impression of the anger when considered in relation to its individual components? Going further, along the lines suggested by the zigzag diagram, what is the anger like, considered in the light of the indefinitely many points of experience (x's, y's, z's, etc.) available to us when we delve into second-level 'time', out of which the first-level experience of anger emerges as the merest superficial expression?

Seen in relation to its first-level fractional components, each one savored with great attentiveness, the solid and heavy second-level feeling of anger or pain has never developed an exclusively angry or painful character. Seen in relation to the infinite zigzag series of 'time' which is available in every presence, the feeling of pain does not even begin to dominate the field of experience, let alone pervade our awareness. And since it does not get the opportunity to claim to be all that is happening, it can never become evidence that the situation is 'bad', 'negative', or 'unpleasant'.

Next, instead of working with such intense situations, consider the large amounts of time which just 'go by', unused in any really creative way because the individual component periods—a few seconds, minutes, or hours here and there—seem intrinsically limited or inadequate for really accomplishing anything. By learning to be sensitive to the infinity of 'time' available within any clock-time period, we can begin to appreciate more fully the value and possibilities life presents. We can begin by noticing more time, more available moments, and then later we can have a more intimate experience with 'time'. 'Time' can become very much a part of us, and can nourish and fulfill us. Finally, with sufficient appreciation of our actually *being* 'time', we—or 'knowingness'—can abide forever within the smallest duration of clock-time.

III

Ordinarily, we have an unfortunate tendency to locate or orient ourselves in a very fixed way. Of course,
we do not see this tendency as being a problem, but
rather a way of keeping ourselves, our self-images, properly defined and grounded. But this self-centeredness ob-
scures the vastness of space and time available by consolidating against it. Time is reduced to mere points in a line,
to a handy and fixed device for keeping track of things
and identities. Time's free and expressive character is reduced to an orderly process of discrete 'things' changing.

By opening up to more time, however, we can have a
more profound type of Time-Space-Knowledge experience. The previous two sections have attempted to facilitate this kind of opening by letting us see more time,
at least in the case where *more time* means a previously
unnoticed series of moments available for having experiences. Two types of such series were discovered to be
accessible. The more obvious was simply the tiny temporal points which, just as a matter of the mathematics of
divisible quantities, constitute any typical temporal interval. A more subtle discovery was the open-ended zigzagging series of points which can be enjoyed, apparently
'between' the beginning and the end of each such linearly
defined interval. These points are potentially infinite in
number and are not quantitatively fixed in duration. Nor
can they be identified with the infinitely divisible fractions
of time which compose a given clock-time interval. They
are not first-level 'points' or fractions of time, but infinitely
expandable moments in a stream of second-level time. The
x's 'between' A and B:

and the y's between any two x's:

y
y   y
X₁   y
y,
y,   X₂
y   y ⁿ y

do not have to be such that the y's are tiny fractional components of longer x-periods.

Now, even though the 'zigzag experience' is more complex in some ways than a simple awareness of smaller fractions of first-level time, this second-level experience also involves a 'knowingness' which can be sensitive to such fractions. In fact, we can not only utilize small intervals like minutes and seconds more successfully (as we did in section II), but we can be aware of the passage of extremely tiny temporal intervals. We can start with the clock-time minute, and with careful attention, notice the passage of the individual seconds that it comprises. As we become adept at that, we can divide each second into ten periods. Continuing this trend, individual milliseconds can eventually be noticed.

As you might point out here, we have already gone beyond what seems possible to modern physiological models of perception. But we are not finished yet. In fact, we have barely begun; this exercise can continue until we can perceive a thousandth of a millisecond. We— or more precisely, 'knowingness'—can then go on to notice a thousandth of that, so that 'we' are tracking billionths of a second. Even then, we can continue.

Now at this point you may feel quite strongly that what is being proposed here is impossible. If so, consider that according to the Time-Space-Knowledge vision, the physiological model of human capacities, according to which *consciousness* is incapable of noticing such tiny intervals, may not be the complete picture. That is, it may not be proper to take this familiar model of the physical basis of consciousness as also being the last word on the basis and capacities of 'knowingness'. The 'knowingness' used in this exercise is not an element of any picture of reality derived from observations performed within ordinary time, and is therefore not something that can be either encompassed by science or possessed by the ego. It is the *ego's* consciousness and capacities, not the full range of *human* capacities and their ground, that are amenable to description by conventional scientific models.

Moreover, your sense that we cannot go beyond a certain point in noticing intervals of time may involve a belief that a certain temporal fraction is experimentally atomic, indivisible, and marked out by precise boundaries. But a close investigation of that allegedly atomic unit interval can show that this is not the case. Can you find defining boundary lines which mark it out and which prevent the observation of its component intervals? If you look closely, you may not find this 'atomic unit'. And just as for this particular interval, so too for any smaller ones you may examine. There is no particular temporal point that is too small to divide when using a more advanced 'know-ingness'.

However, there is a very surprising, even shocking 'end' to this dividing process. For eventually, we may contact temporal fractions which are 'too small', at least for ordinary first-level awareness, or for any vestige of that awareness, with its emphasis on *points*, to remain active. We will then have gone 'beneath' all points, in a sense. Neither first- nor second-level experience, both of which involve a serial unfolding of moments of time, remains. We have, in a manner of speaking, gone 'beneath' all temporal patterning. This is one way of glimpsing Great Time as appreciated by Great Knowledge.

Great Time and Great Knowledge are not condi-tions or positions, but for purposes of explanation, we can loosely speak of the insight available 'from' the vantage point of Great Time and Great Knowledge. 'From' this new vantage, 'beneath' time, we ('knowingness') can see that ordinary consciousness and perceptions, immersed as they are within linear time, are actually out of touch with the living, immediate, and fulfilling character of reality.

Consider the familiar case of seeing stars in the sky. We know that on such occasions we are actually receiving emissions of light from stars and stellar events that have themselves been dead or past for years—perhaps even millions of years. Our customary position in ordinary time and our consciousness give rise to a similar situation: we have contact with *artifacts* rather than the immediacy and central quality of reality. Consciousness is insensitive and yields only indirect, clumsy contact, because it and linear time are viscous, dense, impure. That is, they are not totally frictionless and translucent, and hence are not capable of responsiveness free from distortion and resistance. So no effective contact is available, and the overall course of life does not permit much real achievement, penetration of obstacles, or fulfillment.

Having explained Great Time in this preliminary fashion, we face the interesting but rather paradoxical fact that in what we have called the vantage point 'beneath' ordinary time, we are far removed from ordinary perceptions, sensations, and so on, and yet are more in touch with the core or pith of reality. There is no 'happening', because the time required for 'happenings' does not function, and yet we are in closer contact with that which is reflected in a distorted way when presented as an event or 'happening'.

By working in this new way, we can enjoy the complete emergence of Great Knowledge, a way of knowing that is thoroughly clear and sensitive, untainted by ordinary sensations and discriminations, and yet not at all some kind of 'blank'. Discriminations depend on preferences and dichotomies, and these result from a resistance to phenomena rather than from intimate contact.° How-

---

°See, in this regard, the discussion of 'in' or 'within' found in chapter 14 of *Time, Space, and Knowledge*.

ever, each point in time, including those involving such discriminations, offers the same possibility of contact with Great Time, here conceptualized as being 'beneath' ordinary time. Given the proper appreciation and investigation, it will be found that there is no fundamental taint or characteristic which marks some points as lacking this Great Time dimension or prohibiting contact with it, while marking other points as having this dimension.

The last few ideas above are of the greatest importance for the problem of attaining release from what is traditionally called the "samsaric condition." If it is true that we have access to a 'knowingness' which can reach a subtle 'level' where ordinary time and temporal patterns are inoperative, or not yet developed, then this can explain why release from samsara is *possible*. Moreover, if this release is possible within every particular point of ordinary time, then that fact has tremendously positive implications for the overall status of samsara, which is revealed as an arbitrarily limited orientation rather than a realm clearly demarcated and set in opposition to some 'higher reality'.

We might just quickly point out here that these possibilities also show the way to a new and completely precise account of all physical and mental processes observed on the ordinary level of experience. For, if we can begin in the vantage point entirely 'beneath' ordinary temporal functioning, and observe the subtle patterns which develop out of that and eventually consolidate or 'freeze' into ordinary lawlike patterns and processes, we can rigorously describe, perhaps using mathematics, the nature of these patterns. We can therefore discover the fundamental patternings out of which the first-level perception of 'objects' eventually emerges. The precision and comprehensiveness of this approach—both in its capacity for description and in its predictive power—may go far beyond anything obtainable by ordinary science, which only observes the final, surface stage of this consolidating pattern.

Let us return now to a discussion of what we have been calling the vantage point 'beneath' time. 'From there', it becomes clear that it is absolutely futile to try to resolve our problems by initiating further temporal series—that is, by using up more ordinary time meditating, going somewhere, fixing things, or 'doing' something. All such approaches miss the essential point. However, this new insight also goes beyond the idea that our problems must be solved by retreating to a place 'beneath' time and then staying there. Rather, our previous discussion is simply a first approach toward the accommodation of a vision that shows how we may loosen the knot of our samsaric condition without trying either to untangle it or to cut through it to some other place.

Therefore, hand-in-hand with seeing Great Time as 'beneath', we must realize that there is no ultimate difference between being caught up in ordinary time and being 'beneath' it in Great Time; both are actually of the same nature when seen clearly. But *until* we seek in a new way and get the special flavor of 'underneath', we will not be able to see that this flavor belongs to 'ordinary time' as well. Once we taste it, it catalyzes a transformation in everything; it effects a kind of effortless alchemical transmutation of all reality without transcending anything (in the sense of going somewhere else). Everything is immediately revealed as open, unbinding, and unobscuring, like the clearest and most frictionless of liquids.

To discover this special quality or flavor, we can trace the smallest division of time until the ordinary mind loses all support or possibility of functioning and blows open. This may involve encounters which tentatively suggest a contrast between the resulting type of 'knowing' and ordinary consciousness. But this only indicates how things look when approached in a certain way, rather than establishing an absolute difference—when investigated still more thoroughly—between ordinary consciousness and higher 'knowingness'.

All ordinary perception is pervaded with the same flavor as Great Knowledge. All ordinary temporal intervals also preserve this quality, and the patterns and boundaries which characterize ordinary time and allow us to quantify fixed units of time simply offer boundless possibilities for experience and Being when investigated closely. It is ordinary time which grounds all 'going' from one thing to the next (and therefore all distinctions). For this reason, since we discover Great Time without *going* someplace, we do not use ordinary time, but we also do not set up a distinction between ordinary and Great Time (because such distinctions themselves involve a subtle going 'from' and 'to').

The entire discussion so far obviously applies not only to time but to experience, and we can extend it to include the experiencer as well. Just as we practiced going into points within points, apparently moving further away from the engagements predicated on uncritically contacting ordinary temporal intervals, we also can practice opening up the presence in time of the ordinary subject or knower. That is, we—'knowingness'—can explode each presence of the 'knower' into many zigzagging temporal series, which themselves coalesce around a knowing 'self' and known 'object', until the ordinary emphasis on a knowing self and acts of perception is finally opened up, and Great Time and Great Knowledge clearly emerge.

In this way, pushing further and further back from both surface-level perceptions and the more subtle perceptions that result from 'pushing back', we can contact something that is more truly *present* than are ordinary objects of consciousness. There is no duration remaining in which acts of perception might occur and no fixed place for a 'watcher' to stand: thus, there is no 'experience'. But this third-level appreciation is, as mentioned above, not an absence or a negation, and is not fundamentally different from ordinary time and experience. It is *within* everything. In stepping back and pushing away from experience, we have not *gone* anywhere.

Testing and tasting reality in the ways described in this section can provide direct, tangible evidence for the possibilities discussed. So long as a few basic insights are kept in mind and allowed to guide this exploration, it can lead quickly and directly to discovering the flavor of time and knowledge. All of these points have been discussed in *Time, Space, and Knowledge*, but because of their relevance here, it would be well, in closing, to summarize them.

The first and most central is that we *are* 'time', rather than merely isolated objects located in, but separate from, it. Thus, our experience, too, *is* 'time', and since 'time' has no intrinsic limits, but only artificial or arbitrarily imposed ones, our experience can be infinitely extended. Second, we and our experience are drawn up within 'space' by 'time', and we remain 'space' throughout this expressive play. We are present in a way that remains open, undone.

Third, the play of 'space' and 'time' that embraces our reality is palpably present, 'known', because 'space' and 'time' always bear 'knowledge' or 'knowingness'. The 'knowing self', with its acts of perception, is simply one facet of the field of appearance appreciated by 'knowledge'. Emphasis on the 'self' as the knower does not stray from the primacy of 'knowledge', but does impose arbitrary limits on the extent to which 'knowledge' and appreciation of 'space' and 'time' can be enjoyed. For, by insisting on being the 'knower', the self assumes a position of limited capacity, set apart from the boundless capacity of 'knowledge'.

By releasing our ordinary picture of reality without rejecting or changing it, it can be seen that we are 'space', 'time', and 'knowledge': nothing has ever been otherwise. But this does not mean that in each 'instant' of the linear-time past everything was constituted by 'space', 'time', and 'knowledge' (where these latter are construed as things which are *in* time and which compose everything else). Not at all! When 'knowledge' enjoys the entirety of our present situation as 'space' and 'time', this same 'knowledge' is able to remain undeceived by time's apparent passage: the partitions which mark out discrete temporal points and the feeling of moments having elapsed are recognized as *unreal*. Everything—whether past, present, or future—is seen to be unoriginated, because 'knowledge' perceives that, in point of fact, *there is no moving time*.

Part Two

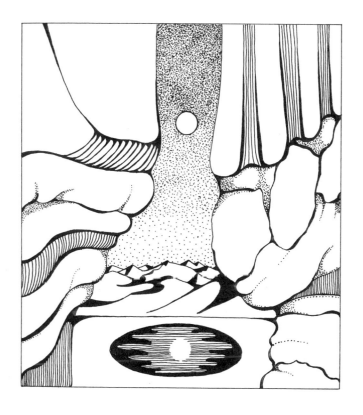

CHAPTER 1

After more than two thousand years, the figure of Socrates remains striking and enigmatic. What are we to make of a cobbler whose greatest delight was to engage with others in contemplating the nature of justice, piety, friendship, love, and so on, let alone one who, still lucid after a long night of drinking and philosophizing, would stand vigil until dawn, waiting for the "voice" that sometimes came to guide him? And how could he have inspired such reverence in Plato, the patriarch of Western philosophy? For Socrates never systematized his thought and appears to have been certain of little save that virtue requires knowledge.

Robert Scharff suggests that Socrates becomes less of a mystery if we realize that he was not primarily concerned with knowledge of the ordinary sort, knowledge that one either 'has', or else lacks and hopes to 'get'. Instead, Dr. Scharff believes, the wisdom that Socrates loved was a 'higher knowingness', "remarkably similar" to that discussed in *Time, Space, and Knowledge*, a kind of "vital understanding" that is, by its nature, essentially incompletable, irreducible to a set of principles, and conducive to an enriched and fully human existence.

The similarities between Great Knowledge and Socratic 'wisdom', as Dr. Scharff describes it, are indeed striking. And if the reader would like to explore his line of thought in more detail, Part Three of *Time, Space, and Knowledge*, the Foreword to this anthology, and "Orientation to Time, Space, and Knowledge" should prove helpful.

The subjects of space, time, and knowledge may seem far removed from the personal and societal issues that occupied Socrates, but they are not. Persons and societies are manifestations of space, time, and knowledge, and thus greater appreciation of these three aspects of reality automatically elicits growth at all levels of human experience. For further exploration of this topic, the reader is referred to the articles by A. Egendorf and J. Shultz.

Robert C. Scharff

A Socratic Approach to
TIME, SPACE, AND KNOWLEDGE

Stated simply, this paper's thesis is that Socrates' philosophizing possesses a remarkable (though not entirely unqualified) kinship with Tarthang Tulku's thinking in *Time, Space, and Knowledge*.[1] But what I want to argue is that special benefits may come from a consideration of this particular kinship, because one must first labor to set it up. According to most of our commentaries, Socrates was, above all, Plato's inspiring teacher—the philosopher who was himself unable to go as far toward ultimate truth as his famous student. However, the Socrates that figures in my thesis is instead a philosopher who, in his single-minded concern for *understanding "how to live"*, never actually shared Plato's dream of *knowing "what is real"*. It is the latter Socrates who, I believe, possesses a remarkable kinship with Tarthang Tulku; and it is therefore through a defense of this Socrates that I will try to set up a discussion of that kinship.

My paper, then, has four parts. Section I indicates how the Western tradition may be read as, above all, a series of responses to the views of Plato. In Section II, I shall argue briefly that insofar as Western philosophers remain in various ways the heirs to a Platonic heritage, the basic intention of Tarthang Tulku's work is likely to elude them. In Section III, I will distinguish Socratic from Platonic philosophizing, along the lines mentioned above. And finally, in Section IV, I will try to show how, in the moment this distinction becomes clear to us, we may recover from within our tradition a long underutilized philosophical orientation which opens us up to *Time, Space, and Knowledge* in a manner that Platonic readings cannot.

Strictly speaking, then, this paper is conceived as both something less and also something more than an exercise in comparative philosophy. It is something less, because Socrates and Tarthang Tulku are not here assumed to be so thoroughly understood as to promote their joint evaluation from a third or neutral viewpoint. But it is also something more, in the sense that the Socrates who emerges from these pages is meant to offer, for contemporary Western thinking, the possibility of a "mediation" between one heritage now experienced with some dissatisfaction and another tradition which, at this late date, we could never swallow whole.

I. Our Platonic Heritage

I begin with a famous story. At the end of one of Plato's early dialogues, a prototypical character named Euthyphro protests that he has no more time to deal with Socrates' questions about piety. The irony of his situation escapes him. He is off to do something pious, still firm in his conviction that he knows what piety is, when the clear evidence of the dialogue implies that he does not. Now, Euthyphro's special brand of religiosity—the particular source of his confidence on this occasion and in connection with this issue—may be unusual. But, alas, his impatience with Socrates is perfectly ordinary. Most people can be expected to take pride in some form of expertise (or even just common sense) which will prompt them to think that they, too, have no time for philosophy and yet are losing nothing of importance on this account.

Supposedly, however, there is another, happier side to this story—a side upon which Plato concentrated in later dialogues. The possibility exists that some few persons may become philosophers anyway. Perhaps inspired by the example of Socrates, or perhaps exposed to the proper education, these few may learn to discount the only apparently authoritative opinions of the impatient many. And in this case, they might then also come to see that the struggle to know, and to speak knowingly of what 'really' is, are the special tasks which exercise the mind in its most excellent condition. Of course, Plato was right. In the long series of responses that followed after his own struggles, the dramatic tale of a few philosophers emerging in the midst of many Euthyphros was repeatedly reenacted.

With the beginning of the modern period, however, the course of this development was altered in a fundamental way. Even in Plato's own philosophizing, one could already discern not only a *metaphysical urge*, an overarching desire to know the really real, but also a *logical demand*, namely, that genuine knowing become self-conscious of itself precisely as the genuine knowing it is. Yet, unfortunately, it became apparent that after Plato, philosophers had only managed to produce a string of 'knowledge claims' that were as much at odds with one another as the 'opinions' of the world's many Euthyphros.

Bacon and Descartes were among the first to give systematic explanations for this embarrassing circumstance. Granted that there is in fact a fundamental difference between metaphysical, or essential, knowledge and mere opinion. Granted also that the former should be universal and beyond dispute. The trouble is that previous philosophers did not stress sufficiently the need for an *epistemology* that could guarantee the acquisition of such knowledge. Something like Plato's logical demand may well entail a theory of what 'knowing' (as opposed to 'having opinions') really is. But when that demand, so to speak, merely accompanies one's metaphysical inquiries, it comes too late. According to Bacon and Descartes, philosophy would henceforth have to *begin* with the proper epistemological theory. For only if the nature of knowing is clearly understood in advance, can the right methods of philosophical reasoning be worked out; and only when philosophers are thereby all set to reasoning alike, can they then be expected to arrive at universal agreement over the same knowledge claims.

For three centuries thereafter, ancient metaphysical dreams and modern epistemological wariness commingled. In each successive philosophy, some theory of genuine knowing, matched with some conception of proper procedure, kept alive the old feeling that philosophers were indeed embarked upon a special and uncommon mission. Among the Continental rationalists and idealists, this sense of mission remained, as it had been for Plato, predominantly *substantive*. That is, in spite of the new concern for method, it still appeared to them that philosophy either inquired after unique topics (e.g., Being, Substance, the Absolute) or, at the very least, had a special slant on otherwise familar topics (e.g., that it knew God by 'reason', established the basic 'principles' for natural science and moral activity, or uncovered the secret 'truth' of human history).

On the other hand, among the Classical empiricists and positivists, the sense of philosophy's mission grew increasingly *methodological*. Embarrassed by their own metaphysical heritage and impressed by the successes of their scientific contemporaries, they became skeptical about philosophy's ability to make substantive contributions of its own. Yet at the same time, the new stress on epistemology left them confident at least of their "knowledge of the nature of knowing"; and this appeared to give them the exclusive right to clarify the concepts and critically assess the arguments which nonphilosophers were too busy using to reflect upon.

So it was that the old Platonic drama continued to unfold under modern conditions. Whether by substantive claim or methodological right, philosophers still represented themselves as occupied with an "extra-ordinary" task. And we might even say that, in point of fact, this drama is still being played out. Especially in the English-speaking world, the majority of philosophers continue to conduct their business as usual, in accordance with yet further refined notions of their special mission. On the one hand, a small band of *speculative* thinkers keeps alive Plato's metaphysical urge. For these contemporary heirs of the oldest traditions, there is still the joy of attempting to frame—though with up-to-date tools and much heightened sense of the dangers involved—a coherent, substantive knowledge system in which every fragment of experience finds its rightful place. On the other hand, there is that much larger collection of *analytical* philosophers who are concerned instead with retelling the modern cautionary tale. No doubt these latter-day epistemologists seem downright anti-Platonic in their preference for our science over ancient cosmology. Nevertheless, they remain—like Bacon and Descartes before them—the heirs to Plato's logical demand, which they now express by crusading for conceptual clarity and rigorous argument.

However, increasingly since the beginning of the present century, there have been some who could not entirely suppress the feeling that Western philosophy, especially since its modern development, has taken on the air of a kind of bad apologetics. To those who have experienced this feeling, the situation appears roughly as follows: With every new speculative vision and at every fresh analytical turn, there seems quickly to have arisen yet another breed of impatient nonphilosophers who already know better what there really is, how to handle it, and with what expected results. Like Plato's Euthyphro, these experts also claim to need no philosophy. Yet unlike Plato's prototype, these latter-day Euthyphros appear to have grown up.

That is, unlike the rather simple and provincial Athenian folk whom Socrates easily embarrassed, but also unlike the dogmatic theological loyalists from whom Bacon and Descartes sought distance, the present century's Euthyphros appear to have matured into scientists and engineers and captains of industry who *really* know what they are doing and therefore *really* have no need for philosophy.

Put in its baldest form, then, the question which haunts some would-be contemporary philosophers is this: Are our grown-up Euthyphros perhaps no longer Euthyphros at all? Are they, instead, the true heirs to philosophy itself—whichever way its special mission is construed? On the one hand, is not their science and their technological savvy obviously superior to ancient or modern metaphysics? On the other hand, insofar as they are now regularly educated to appreciate conceptual clarity, rigorous argument, and careful methodology, are they not then perfectly capable of being their own knowledge analysts? In short, is not philosophy, as the West has thus far experienced it, really and deservedly coming to an end?

M ost contemporary philosophers, of course, would deny all this. Speculative thinkers regard their systems as in principle more comprehensive than modern science could ever be. And analytical thinkers not unreasonably assume that most people will always be too lazy, too busy, or otherwise disinclined to act as their own epistemological critics. Nevertheless, among the relatively smaller group of thinkers who take the matter of philosophy's ending seriously, there is one type—found mainly in the Marxist and existentialist camps—that is especially worth mentioning here. Oversimplifying a great deal, we summarize its outlook as follows: Suppose today's experts are given the benefit of every doubt. Suppose their science does or will supercede speculation; and suppose they do not, or soon will not, need the services of a special class of analytical consultants. Where in such an ending of the grand Western tradition could one find anything like a matured version of that ancient interest in the "good life" and human "excellence" that Socrates deemed infinitely more important than knowledge of the cosmos? Where, in other words, is there room now for what Marxists call a "concern for praxis" which does not reduce to "applied science"? And where are the champions now of what the existentialists refer to as "authentic existence"?

These questions should remind us that when Socrates challenged Euthyphro to tell him of piety, it was above all because Socrates wished to be "virtuous." Reviewed with this in mind, Plato's little story seems to be not so much about the irony of Euthyphro's boastful knowledge claims, but rather about their tragic implication. For in the end, this self-styled expert rushes off to prosecute his father—without ever seriously having asked himself whether that is what he should do. Perhaps we should say, then, that his impatience with Socrates would be more amusing if it were not so dangerous. And in that case, it may be that what haunts the thoughts of those Marxists and existentialists just mentioned is a danger of the same kind, but of infinitely greater proportions. For it seems as if they are asking: "In a world which lacks a Socrates, where philosophy is ending amidst speculative and analytical attempts to know more and argue better, can we really have much confidence in today's experts being any more careful in their actions than the overconfident Euthyphro?" As we shall see, this does not quite recapture the Socratic spirit or its kinship with *Time, Space, and Knowledge*, but it may encourage us to do so.

II. Misunderstanding TIME, SPACE, AND KNOWLEDGE Platonically

In his preface to *Time, Space, and Knowledge*, Tarthang Tulku explains that

> the general language and style of philosophy seemed most appropriate for this initial presentation; it allows the possibility of presenting a vision which begins on the level of reason and analysis, and then grows and opens within itself. Such a rational, systematic investigation can contribute to a meditative exploration, and is actually essential if we are to appreciate our full value as human beings. (p. xxxiv)°

Now such a work may hold great promise—but not if its "general language and style" is interpreted immediately in accordance with one of the contemporary attitudes deriving from our Platonic heritage.

On the one hand, the "vision" to which Tarthang Tulku refers is not *speculative* in our sense. Even if he repeatedly associates that vision with a kind of "higher knowledge," a knowledge which he also describes on occasion as necessary "in order to comprehend . . . the unity of Being" (p. 293; cf. p. xxv and p. 291), this does not

---

°This and all the parenthetical page references that follow are to *Time, Space, and Knowledge.*—ED

mean he is producing a new ontology or cosmology. One would examine *Time, Space, and Knowledge* in vain for any version of a Platonic *eidos* or Aristotelian *arché* which fixes contemplatively or explains metaphysically the phenomenal particulars of ordinary experience and scientific research.

On the other hand, the very fact that Tarthang Tulku speaks of "higher" knowledge at all is likely to provoke *analytical* misunderstandings. In our predominantly anti-metaphysical age, we can well imagine the typical reaction: first, chauvinistic remarks about the Orient's failure to produce Science; and then, protestations against muddled concepts, faulty arguments, and mysticism's general disrespect for Real Life. From such a viewpoint, even Tarthang Tulku's warning—namely, that the virtually universal presumption in favor of common sense and scientific theory is precisely what blocks the way to the Time-Space-Knowledge vision—will no doubt be used against him.

In short, we must expect that *Time, Space, and Knowledge* will get sympathetically misread by today's speculative thinkers, and barely read at all by our contemporary analysts of concept and argument. But how, then, should the work be approached?

Perhaps the best thing to note first is that Tarthang Tulku's conception of "reason and analysis" is fundamentally nontheoretical. I mean to make the following contrast: as traditionally understood, metaphysical and ethical reasoning are supposed to establish, respectively, a comprehensive theory of the real and a set of moral directives. Yet, the whole history of these philosophical efforts has been haunted by the embarrassing fact that one can evidently remain insensitive to, or even willfully ignore, their results. Alas, according to the cliché, theory is one thing and practice another. It is with this in mind that I call Tarthang Tulku's "reason and analysis" nontheoretical. For in his conception, these are interpretive or therapeutic powers whose very employment effects a transformation of the manner in which one lives and acts. Hence, there can in principle be no moment when the 'results' of their employment are already clear, but one must still decide whether and how to 'use' them.

Briefly summarized, the interpretive transformation recounted in *Time, Space, and Knowledge* proceeds as follows: First, our conventional ways of experiencing and knowing are analyzed in order to uncover in them certain congealed and self-perpetuating patterns. Here the aim is neither to prove these patterns conceptually muddled, nor to establish their metaphysical ground, nor to clear the way for moral advice. The point is rather to "thaw them out" (see, e.g., 240ff.)—that is, to show that just by bringing these patterns into focus, in precisely the forms in which we live through them, it is possible to realize their ultimately unsatisfying character. But next, the very fact that this unsatisfactoriness can be realized and thought about is taken to be already the beginning of a movement toward more adequate "higher knowingness." At this stage, the aim is not to contemplatively transcend common sense or meta-theorize over scientific understanding. The point is rather to open up these conventional ways of experiencing and thinking into a higher knowingness—to transform them, as Tarthang Tulku says, by a "rational, systematic investigation" which in turn "contributes to a meditative exploration."

Hence, if this transformation does eventually reveal our conventional ways to be "lower knowingness", it emphatically does not involve their being either left behind or supplemented by another separate kind of experiencing and knowing. On the contrary, they are retained precisely as imperfect expressions of that same higher knowingness which, in turn, is now understood to have been vitally operative all along—even though at first it could only make its presence felt as an unexplored dimension of unsatisfactoriness in our familiar activities.

In short, "reason and analysis" in *Time, Space, and Knowledge* are neither speculatively motivated nor do they break off when some mystical punch line is about to be delivered. True enough, the text distinguishes "meditative exploration" from "rational investigation." But it also says the latter *contributes* to the former. Hence, "reason and analysis" cannot be wholly associated with either lower or higher knowledge. Rather they are, strictly speaking, integral to the entire process of transformation; and one might therefore say of them what Tarthang Tulku says of the Time-Space-Knowledge vision, namely, that it both *"grows and opens within itself"* and also facilitates appreciation of "our full value *as human beings*."

All this, of course, is as easy to describe as it is difficult to fathom—which accounts for the double reference to "meditative" and "rational" activity, as well as for the thirty-five "exercises" interspersed throughout the text. Yet so much, at least, is clear: to the extent that speculative philosophy wants a theory of the real and analytical philosophy simply means to make us better reasoners, they both face away from the central concern in *Time, Space, and Knowledge*. If one wants to give this book a proper hearing, the question to ask is this: How does one go about developing a vision which, by "growing and opening within itself," *at the same time* moves one toward an enriched and more fully human existence?

Now mightn't this question catch the interest of the sort of Marxists and existentialists mentioned in the previous section? After all, they are obviously opposed to the prospect of still more speculative and analytical business as usual. And their various politico-economic and moral critiques of contemporary life seem clearly to be ruled by a desire for something better. So might we not expect them to give a receptive hearing to a work that not only stands entirely outside the dominant Western tradition, but also states explicitly that its "basic intention" is "to encourage a new and more fulfilling approach to life"? (p. xxxiv) The answer, I think, has to be no.

My question here is not the empirical one of how many Marxist and existentialist thinkers actually are or will be sympathetic to extra-Western works. Rather, I want to suggest that in principle and despite appearances, these thinkers are committed by fundamental intuition to an outlook that fosters still another misreading of *Time, Space, and Knowledge*. To see why, let us return for a moment to Plato's *Euthyphro*.

As indicated earlier, the implicit tragedy (as opposed to the explicit irony) of this little story lies in the fact that Euthyphro's impatience with Socrates' questions leads us to expect him to follow an unjust course of action. In order to graphically depict what may be the core intuition of some Marxist and existentialist writers, we imagined them varying this theme by substituting contemporary scientific understanding for Euthyphro's peculiar religiosity, so that the whole Western world (including most of its "philosophers") is made to appear fundamentally insensitive to Socratic questions. In a world thus "grown up", all the obvious answers for "What is the good life?" would derive from applied science. And this, to follow our imaginative variation to the bitter end, virtually guarantees perpetuating human misery and injustice (not to mention precipitating ecological disaster) on a grand scale.

But now notice the conceptual corner into which this imagery paints us. Try really imagining a *Euthyphro*-like tragedy writ large across our world. And then try asking what sort of latter-day Socrates would stand any chance of revealing the enormity of such a problem, and who would be his willing foils. In other words, contrast our situation, so imagined, with the Athens of Plato's childhood; and ask, in each case, how promising are the prospects for "wisdom."

Socrates, we are told, could actually "love" wisdom. This means, first, that he was able to distinguish it clearly from natural knowledge on the one hand and from poetry and technical skillfulness on the other. And this in turn means, second, that he was able to pursue it with single-minded devotion, directly and unceasingly over almost half a century, for the sake of the compelling higher question of the good life. Indeed, it even seems fair to say that Socrates was more enlightened than deterred in this pursuit by his confrontations with the nonwisdom which surrounded him.

But who among today's tragic-minded radicals pursues an analogous course? And from whom might they even learn that there is one? In other words, if the whole world has become the living expression of Plato's little story, what hope is there of anyone growing to love Socratic wisdom? And further and far worse, what difference would it make if anyone ever did?

The terrifying implication of these questions is, I think, what haunts the iconoclastic, rebellious, and anxiously untimely thoughts of many contemporary Marxists and existentialists; and this effectively short-circuits any possibility of their either developing a genuinely Socratic viewpoint or turning receptively toward works like *Time, Space, and Knowledge*. With all their dialectical skill and vital resolve, they must remain above all foes of modern nonwisdom, for whom the ancient ideal of the good life can only survive in obscure and infertile allusions to "species being" and "authentic existence." This is, of course, completely understandable. For how else, except through such allusions, might they express their deepest feeling, namely, that what is really needed is at the same time entirely out of present reach? But understandable though this feeling may be, it is equally clear that, like Socrates, Tarthang Tulku most emphatically does not share it. Hence one must expect *Time, Space, and Knowledge* to be misperceived as hopelessly escapist and Panglossian by those who do.

III. Socratic Philosophizing Recovered

But let us see now if we can bring Socrates' philosophizing more directly into focus—without either speculative or analytical presumptions, and also without becoming distracted by polemics against them. In simplest terms, our procedure will be to acknowledge that both the Platonic metaphysical urge and its accompanying logical demand are absent from Socrates' pursuit of wisdom. But where traditional interpretations have in various ways held this against him, we shall argue on the contrary that it is a clue to his success. A detailed review of these interpretations is out of the question here; but a few remarks about their basic orientation will be useful.

Perhaps the most widely shared feature of the common accounts of Socrates is their stress upon the unsatisfactory nature of his supposed claim that "virtue is knowledge." Actually, a whole nest of "paradoxes" has been perceived here, but reduced to its essentials, the problem is this: by all accounts, Socrates was in fact a virtuous man. Yet although he taught that there is a kind of higher knowledge which makes such virtue possible, at the same time, in all the early Platonic dialogues where the historical Socrates himself is speaking, he consistently denies having this knowledge. Hence, there is the paradox of the virtuous man who lacked the knowledge needed to make him so.

Now in general, attempts to deal with this paradox have worked primarily upon either Socrates' conception of *knowledge* or his confessions of *ignorance*. According to the former approach, his doctrine is not nearly so puzzling if one refrains from measuring it against excessively rigorous and post-Socratic conceptions of what knowledge is. Hence, one must remember that when Socrates asked his "What is *X*?" questions, he was only interested in some particular topic (e.g., piety, courage, or justice) and not in comprehensively grasping them all. Moreover, it seems clear that even with regard to a particular topic, he was willing to settle for considerably less than what we would now call an "essential" (or universal) definition.

In fact, however, this approach is rarely pursued for Socrates' benefit. Interpreters who take this line are usually just preparing the ground for their accounts of Plato's more admirable and ambitious program, in which all "What is *X*?" questions really do point toward *the* question of the Good or the One. Certainly it is no vindication of Socrates' own pursuit of wisdom to say that his best student's metaphysics was extrapolated from it.

In order, then, to give Socrates himself a fairer hearing, many commentators have stressed the need to analyze what he actually did, instead of wondering immediately about its metaphysical outcome. And obviously the one thing he always seemed to do was begin his inquiry with a genuine confession of ignorance. Of course, the fact that all

learning depends upon a willingness to say "I don't already know" and mean it, has long since become everyone's truism. Yet Socrates was certainly the pioneering
genius here; and even today, his various ways of making
this point still have a special power to illuminate its complexity and difficulties.

So much, at least, is rightly stressed. But problems arise
for this approach, too, when it becomes evident that
behind Socrates' confessions of ignorance, there seemed
to lie some very untentative convictions. Among other
things, he consistently maintained that cosmology can
never clarify moral issues; that unjust action is always
wrong, even in the face of unjust treatment; and that
caring for the soul is always superior to caring for material
well-being. In short, Socrates frequently appears to have
known a great deal; and this raises doubts about the sin-
cerity of his confessions.

Some have sought to dispel these doubts by arguing
that Socratic confession is often "ironic," that is, involves
legitimate and pedagogically motivated withholding of
presumed knowledge, for the sake of engaging interlocutors in mutually beneficial dialogue. Others have suspect-
ed something less admirable, namely, a deliberate feigning
of ignorance, for the purpose of eventually shocking or
embarrassing a dogmatic or closed-minded dialogue partner. But neither explanation is very satisfying. Construe
Socrates' confessions as ironic, and obviously the next
question will be the proto-Platonic one, namely, what
was the nature and extent of the knowledge which, for
whatever reason, he withheld from view. Construe his

confessions as feints, and he becomes difficult to distinguish from that deceitful and manipulative "debater" his enemies took him to be.

In short, it seems that a 'defense' of Socrates' philosophy, even if it begins by stressing his procedure instead of his opinions, must still inevitably take comfort from the fact that it stimulated Plato's *metaphysical* urge. Or else, it must become an entirely different kind of defense, namely, one in which neither Socrates' own inquiries nor his inspiring of Plato, but rather just his procedural contribution to modern *epistemology* is made the central topic. In fact, I think, this latter sort of defense has today become the most popular. And that brings me to the point of this extremely condensed review.

What seems most apparent about the usual interpretations of Socrates is that they make either substantive or methodological assumptions which, while "obvious" for everyone today, inevitably leave his philosophizing in an only partially respectable position. Speculatively or metaphysically construed, Socrates is only praised for having sought what others would have to find. Analytically or epistemologically evaluated, he gets a few good marks because he stressed the need for open-mindedness and candid questioning—which, of course, are seen as mere preliminaries in some correct and more fully determined modern theory of knowledge.

But against these interpretations, let me now ask: Is it right to assume that all 'knowledge' is, analogous with the metaphysico-speculative kind, something one either *has*, or hopes to have, or should otherwise confess not having? Must every admission of ignorance therefore be construed correlatively as an instance of (possible or definite) *not knowing*? Through my alternative interpretation, I want to suggest that Socrates can still show us how to answer these questions in the negative.

To summarize this interpretation in advance: I see Socrates' confessions of ignorance as his way of staying in touch with a kind of *vital understanding*, the precise nature of which defies our usual speculative and analytical conceptions of 'knowledge', 'tentative' knowledge, and 'lack' of knowledge. This understanding is most appropriately described as something like a single, seamless, reflectively stimulated process in which a *given* sense of how to live is *continually* tested against new experiences, with a full recognition that it is essentially *incompletable*. Let us consider each of these three characteristics in turn.

1. That Socratic inquiries emerge from and depend upon some *given understanding* may be explained in two parts. In the first place, even those persons who have never cared to raise the question "How shall I live?" are already, so to speak, expressing their careless answers to it with every word and deed. Behaving thus "unwisely" is, of course, exactly what Socrates was pledged to avoid. Yet, the general question of how to live is, as such, never what he asks. Instead, in each inquiry, he focuses attention upon one of its many aspects by formulating a particular sort of "What is *X*?" question, for example, about piety, courage, or justice. And so it happens that each of his actual inquiries is still, at bottom, expressive of his unflagging concern for the general issue of how to live.

But second, if this is the case, we need to have a clear picture of the characteristic relationship which obtains between Socrates' particular questions and his fundamental one. Of course, on any reading, the former questions obviously never arise in a vacuum, with nothing to go on; some 'answer' to the questioned X is always presupposed. But according to the usual interpretations, this can only mean that what is presupposed is some alleged 'knowledge', which Socrates initially withholds or renders tentative through a confession of ignorance. On such a view, each confession becomes a kind of theoretically heuristic device, motivated by intellectual curiosity or wonder, and expressive of a desire to know (or make sure he already knows) the essential idea or principle of the questioned X.

In my opinion, however, this cannot be right. If Socrates is basically interested in how to live, and if what he calls "knowing" (i.e., being "wise") is tantamount to being virtuous, then he could never settle for knowing and testing 'principles'. For as everyone is painfully aware, principles may be "had" without getting applied. Hence, in my view, Socrates does not ask his "What is X?" questions against the background of any presupposed 'knowledge'. Rather, he sees them as emerging from what we might call a kind of 'lived understanding' which is neither reducible to any principle or set of principles nor even exhaustively analyzable in terms of the particular X in question. As I conceive it, this understanding quite generally determines, for us as for him, "how one is disposed" toward every vital issue, including the present one. In other words, I take it here to be no more and no less than his current overall outlook on the problem of how to live. Keeping this in mind, we can resolve a number of issues.

For one thing, it is hardly surprising that Socrates should make the condition of this general understanding a matter of such urgent concern. For unlike a theory or principle which one might just consider intellectually without applying, this vital sense of things is precisely what is always 'enacted'. Thus, instead of saying he 'has it', we might better describe it as 'possessing him'—both in the sense that it covers too much to be considered all at once, and also in the sense that it always already constitutes what he 'really thinks', without his ever having planted it there by an explicit decision. But this description must not be heard deterministically. For while one's understanding can never be considered *in toto*, traded in, refuted, replaced, and so on, like a principle or theory, it can most certainly be improved. And that, in sum, is just what a Socratic confession of ignorance acknowledges. By making such a confession, he is simply recognizing the need, on this occasion and in relation to one particular topic *X*, to ask how well or how badly he is already "given to understand" (and thus also inclined to act with regard to) this *X*.

2. From all of this it follows that each Socratic inquiry should be interpreted as one singly focused attempt to effect the *continuous improvement* of a multifaceted vital understanding. To explain this point, I turn briefly to the passage in Plato's *Apology* where Socrates recalls how the Delphic Oracle, by declaring that "no one is wiser," led him to understand more fully the meaning of wisdom. The moral of his little story is, of course, well-known. What we must do here is reconstruct the process by which he learned it.

Let us say that, at the outset, Socrates had (i) a pre-Delphic understanding of his philosophical activity, (ii) a message from Apollo he found hard to handle, and therefore (iii) a particular question, namely, "What is wisdom?" In other words, (i) as he already understood the matter, wisdom is not what cosmologists seek or he had found, but rather what politicians, poets, and artisans appeared to have. Yet (ii) in the face of their apparent superiority, the Oracle insisted no one was wiser than he; and in his surprise, Socrates misheard this as "I am the wisest." About this mishearing we shall say more in a moment, but the first point to stress is that he does not begin his inquiry by treating either his current conception of wisdom or Apollo's misheard message as something to be accepted or rejected outright. Instead, he brings (i) his pre-Delphic understanding to bear on (ii) what it cannot handle and (iii) asks: "Once again, what is wisdom? If it is neither what cosmologists seek nor what I have, then how can I still be wiser than all those persons who claim to possess it? Perhaps if I ask them to tell me what they know, I may at least clarify how we differ with regard to wisdom, and at best find the very thing the Oracle is strangely willing to attribute to me."

In the end, however, Socrates found that the attribution had not been so strange after all. From his discussions, he came to see that neither the politicians' savvy and status, nor the poets' skill and reputation, nor the artisans' expertise and material success had anything to do with the 'higher' wisdom he sought; and he came to realize also that he was better off than them for having seen this. In short, Socrates gradually came to understand wisdom better, by seeing how much more he really achieved, in his willingness to forgo any claims to it, than he had at first understood.

Now so far, I have been treating the whole expanse of Socrates' post-Delphic philosophizing as if it were an instance writ large of his more narrowly focused inquiries, that is, as if it were entirely concerned with the question "What is wisdom?" In one sense, of course, this analogy is quite wrong. Socrates' actual dialogues with politicians, poets, and artisans always deal explicitly with something more specific than wisdom as such, for example, justice, courage, piety, or friendship. But surely these are not matters extrinsic to wisdom. On the contrary, they are precisely what a seeker of wisdom inquires about. They are the X's, so to speak, of Socrates' "What is X?" questions, and the clarification of wisdom is always furthered in each one.

Hence, the point of my analogy is this: there is a continuity between Socrates' explicit questions which would remain unexplained if one simply strung them together serially across the course of his career. *Wisdom* is apparently nothing other than Socrates' blanket term for what we earlier called "understanding [truly] how to live." And if the "search after" or "love of" wisdom (i.e., literally, *philosophy*) is therefore just shorthand for his "unflagging concern to meet every occasion as a chance to improve some aspect of that vital understanding," then it follows that Socrates' seemingly separate inquiries should be construed as decisively joined together (from below, so to speak) into one continuous, wisdom-seeking activity.

Perhaps in part because we so often want answers which in fact or in principle settle this question or that, and perhaps also because our many experts (including speculative and analytical philosophers) encourage us to look for such 'knowing' answers, we mostly tend to overlook the possibility of following so continuous and integrated a Socratic path. But Socrates himself had no such problem. Thus, when the Oracle told him there was "no one wiser," he gauged this candidly as a direct and surprising challenge to the whole condition of his vital understanding ("I am the wisest!"). Recognizing that, as a challenge, it could hardly be an "answer" which "settled" anything, he turned it into a question ("How can I still be the wisest, if . . . ?"). But instead of imagining that this general question could itself be immediately addressed all at once, he made it the implicit concern of a whole integral series of inquiries ("Tell me what wisdom you have . . ."). And only after he had pursued them all and his sense of what it is to care about improving one's vital understanding had gradually become clearer, did he then transform his initial question into a *summary report* of what he now realized ("I am indeed, as anyone else like me would also be, the wisest man in this crowd of self-deluded experts").

This report exemplifies as well as anything could, I think, Socrates' own awareness of the unbroken continuity in his process of understanding. Retrospectively, it gathers up the lessons of his earlier inquiries; and prospectively, it leaves him open for future inquiries by stopping short of any overconfident 'definition' of wisdom. Yet, careful inspection reveals that this silent reticence is not quite absolute. For in declaring he is an example of the wisest sort of person, Socrates does not merely compare himself with false claimants; he also suggests that no one will ever be wiser than a Socratic inquirer! This far from self-evident suggestion brings us to the third and final part of my discussion.

3. Stated simply, the reason there can never be "totally wise" persons is that the Socratic task of improving one's understanding is *necessarily incompletable*. This point will become clear, I think, if we return one final time to the *Apology*'s summary report and explain both why and to what extent its account of wisdom, though not definitive, is nevertheless satisfying.

That this report is not definitive must surely be obvious enough. One looks in vain to it for anything like an essential description of wisdom's true nature. But it should be equally obvious what keeps it from being definitive, namely, that it is designed to answer the question "What is wisdom?" only insofar as it was concretely raised by the Oracle's surprising challenge ("No one is wiser") to Socrates' then current understanding ("I lack wisdom"). Hence, the question does get answered—not definitively, but just as soon as he was able to take the initially surprising word of the Oracle into account together with what he had already understood ("I am indeed better off than the politicians, etc., in being aware of my ignorance, and I now realize what Apollo meant . . ."). In short, this question received the same sort of satisfying answer as is possible for his particular "What is X?" questions. Some claim about, or activity involving this or that X (e.g., piety, courage, justice, but here also wisdom) is experienced as surprising, puzzling, challenging—in a word, admittedly questionable because not understood. And an inquiring response continues until just the very thing about X that was initially made questionable is satisfactorily understood.

It is, of course, precisely because we could find a crucial point in Socrates' career when a specific claim about wisdom itself surprised him, that we were able to make "What is wisdom?" analogous to his "What is X?" questions. But as we saw, there comes a point where this analogy breaks down. In its fullest meaning, "What is wisdom?" turns out to be equivalent to "How shall I live?" This, we noted, is really *the* question for Socrates and so cannot be made analogous to any one or any series of "What is X?" questions. Unlike the latter, it cannot even have their carefully circumscribed sort of satisfying answer, let alone a definitive one—for the simple reason that, as *the* question with which each of Socrates' more specialized inquiries is always in some concrete way concerned, it is itself never raised.

But far more important is the fact that it *must not* be raised. If the 'general topic' which informs it is to remain a 'vital' one, the only appropriate way to address it is in terms of a currently given understanding that is challenged by a heretofore unconsidered speaking or acting with regard to some X—an X which thus, on this occasion and in this specifically challenging manner, admittedly requires reexamination and improved understanding. On the other hand, even if there could be a general answer to "What is wisdom?" that answer could never tell us how it presently matters.

Hence, it is precisely by refusing to let this question arise in any other than an implicit and determinately X-oriented way that Socrates guarantees, for the sake of this occasion and all those yet to come, the possibility of existentially satisfying answers. Of course, such answers are not definitive, that is, complete and comprehensive; because so long as there is still a next occasion, the process of vitally understanding, that is, of becoming wise, not only is, but must be incompletable. Small wonder, then, that Socrates should be so certain that there can never be "totally wise" persons. For given the question he wants to raise and the concretely challenging 'forms' he realizes it must always take, the very urge to total wisdom is wholly inappropriate.

In a word, definitive answers are not something Socrates fails to get: they are precisely what he is wise enough not to want. Whether the vitally interesting X's he inquired about even have 'essential definitions' is a matter we cannot pursue here. What is clear is that it could have made no difference to him if they do. Definitive answers are what one might want, at last, to *know*. But Socratic answers are simply what we need, on this occasion, to *understand*. And as long as we are alive, there must be ever-improved formulations of the latter. In a way, then, it is still something of a Platonic insult to call Socrates' process of understanding "incompletable." That there is no definitive Socratic knowledge does not mean he was too preoccupied with concrete cases to be a successful metaphysician. It means he did not seek such knowledge at all. And if he was right in this, it is surely unfortunate that we find it so difficult to 'understand' why.

IV. From Socrates to TIME, SPACE, AND KNOWLEDGE

N ow, to what extent does this discussion of Socratic philosophizing prepare us for *Time, Space, and Knowledge*? Does Tarthang Tulku perhaps also speak from something like the 'vital understanding' we have found in Socrates' inquiries, when he concerns himself with "presenting a vision which . . . grows and opens within itself" and is thereby capable of "inspiring a broad, open-ended, and vigorous appreciation of life"? Certainly there is an apparent affinity here. But to establish any really substantial kinship, we must review the essential features of Socratic 'understanding' directly in terms of the three major themes of *Time, Space, and Knowledge*.

1. *Great Space*, in its most luminous envisionment, is described by Tarthang Tulku as that manifest "openness" which allows us to fully "appreciate what is 'here'." Whatever else may be said negatively and along the way about this openness, its realization is above all linked with a "shift in perspective that has vast lived significance"—significance which is further characterized as allowing us to

> completely transcend a self-centered orientation and become fully *with* everyone and everything else. Locations and attitudes, problems and confusions, no longer bind us. They are seen as a beautiful play of Great Space (without Great Space being viewed as the external creator of the

play). Life and death also provide an interesting play without binding our possibilities in any way. We have no improvement orientation, and yet are fully available to help other people—or to improve things—by phrasing and exemplifying our appreciation of perfection in terms of others' improvement-oriented views. (pp. 113–14)

Now it seems to me that this is precisely what happens *wherever* Socratic philosophizing occurs. Certainly Socrates had no "improvement orientation," for he sought neither increased knowledge nor better material circumstances. It is true that I have, perhaps unfortunately, made continuous improvability one characteristic of his process of understanding. But when this is heard together with my descriptions of its other two characteristics, it should be clear that I was trying to make a very different point, namely, that for Socrates, the deepest appreciation of any *X* experienced 'here' depends on treating his *given* understanding as neither sacrosanct nor moving toward perfect *completeness*.

Hence, Socrates' aim on each occasion is not to understand 'better and better'; rather it is to satisfactorily understand 'again'. And this, it seems to me, is just what made it possible for him to be "fully available" to whomever and whatever he presently experienced. Then, too, it is surely by adopting this same openness of spirit in every dialogue that Socrates repeatedly offered, even for those who were oblivious to it, a chance to take their own unchallenged presumptions less seriously than whatever *X* was there for vitally enriching appreciation. Thus does he speak only ironically of his poverty, and more seriously of his divine mission, and so puzzlingly without fear about death as well as life. And these are some of the reasons why

I want to say that 'wherever' there is Socratic philosophizing, there is envisionment of that Great Space which "provides the opportunity to open up everything. . . ."

2. Equally important for Tarthang Tulku is the fact that "all the activity and characteristics of this opening" are traceable to *Great Time* (p. 211). In the phrasing of *Time, Space, and Knowledge,* to experience the "perfect intimacy" involved here between Space and Time is precisely to move within a vision that is alive to whatever on this occasion is opened up to us as a presence.

> 'Time's' dynamism may then be appreciated as expressing the open accommodation of Great Space. More precisely, *the presentation is itself* the appreciation of 'time' as being allowed by Space and as in turn expressing Space. No additional *act* of appreciation is required. (p. 145)

Again, this seems to describe exactly what happens *whenever* Socratic philosophizing occurs. In order to defend Socrates against interpreters who would divide his life into a series of failed attempts at knowledge, we turned the whole course of his activities into one continuous and ever incompletable process of understanding. There is no need to conceptually 'unify' this process from without; for its continuity and incompletability can already be made fully intelligible in terms of what, on each occasion, he did again, namely, allow what offered itself up to him to become really understood. Tarthang Tulku says one might call these attempts to conceptually 'unify' this process from without a "timing," but he adds that this label still defers too much to views which make 'moments' into parts of a temporal chain which have to be nailed down or else they pass away. Socrates, clearly, would have agreed. For he did not fix occasions in this way, or 'measure' presentations, or 'make' issues out of what he experienced, so as to avoid being overwhelmed by them. Instead he simply let himself be available, understandingly, to whatever there was open, 'here'. And if, at the beginning of each of his inquiries, there is no evidence of any special effort to recall and utilize established principles or push aside previous mistakes, that only shows how, in Tarthang Tulku's phrasing, "no additional *act* of appreciation" was required for him.

3. Finally, then, we must consider the suggestion that *when Space and Time are directly appreciated, that is automatically [Great] Knowledge"* (p. 216). Tarthang Tulku has much to say about this triple-faceted vision *as* a vision, about its illuminating the "unity of Being," and so on. Yet in no sense does this mean he is promoting a theory for application to practice, or a creed to be followed with conviction. Indeed, such conceptions put the matter exactly backwards. As *Time, Space, and Knowledge* repeatedly emphasizes, it is by *"living* the Space-Time-Knowledge vision, . . . [that] we can find the way to our *Being"* (p. 293; emphasis added). And the only way to live this vision at all is to begin with whatever 'knowingness' we already ordinarily live by and let it "grow and open within itself." Experientially speaking, then, Great Knowledge is 'perfect knowing*ness*', not absolute *knowledge*; and since every occasion is once again an opportunity for realizing this, at least to some extent, it is correct to say that

> Great Knowledge grows, not by making linear progress, but by opening up to the infinite perfection that is 'here'. Knowledge commands Space and Time, so this type of 'growth without going anywhere' is possible. (p. 216)

Here, it seems to me, lies the final and deepest kinship between *Time, Space, and Knowledge* and my recovered Socrates. What Tarthang Tulku calls "growth," I find also in Socratic inquiries. For wherever and whenever they take place, their point is always to "come to fully appreciate" *whatever* 'here' is openly encountered—and when that happens, there is "automatically" satisfactory understanding. Thus, on each occasion, Socrates was once again engaged in answering: "Space and Time may play, but who would know it?" (p. 220) One need not be bothered by the abstractness of this question, for Socrates himself had a general name for the task embodied in it. He called it *philosophy*—a "love" of "wisdom" which can "satisfy" itself on each occasion with regard to this determinate aspect of some *X*, but then has to confess on the next one that inquiry must begin again. Such continually re-satisfied understanding is indeed, then, a "growth without going anywhere"; but for just that reason it always is, as Tarthang Tulku says of perfect knowingness, *"too complete* [here] *to be* [in some fixed, transcendent sense] *an accomplishment"* (p. 287). Taking a passage out of context, but perhaps not so radically distorting its meaning, these are indeed

> bold claims, and such a vision may seem very inaccessible. But the way to understand it is not to force some special experience, but simply to relate to what Space and Time continually display. (p. 253)

This, I think, is what Socrates lived by and what the more metaphysically minded Plato began to forget.

However, this last remark should also remind us that kinships, after all, are relations between *different* persons,

and our discussion must make some belated effort to acknowledge this. On the one hand, if I have found Tarthang
Tulku helpful in explicating the inner dynamics of
Socratic philosophizing, that only underscores how little
Socrates himself succeeded in warning us against metaphysically misreading him. On the other hand, I have
entirely ignored the fact that the Time-Space-Knowledge
vision is worked out primarily against conventional views
about the material world, whereas Socrates turned very
early in his career toward moral issues instead. According
to Tarthang Tulku,

> we ordinarily try to *achieve* knowledge in what we see as
> basically an insentient world. This has the effect of freezing
> knowingness into a world of knowable or known but un-
> knowing things. The result is a severe deformation of the
> capacity which is most central to human beings—the capa-
> city to appreciate and enjoy the freshness and fullness of the
> play of Space and Time. (p. 220)

To the extent that one can see the Western tradition as having followed out this deforming achievement, it would
seem fitting to work through the meditative exercises
in *Time, Space, and Knowledge* in order to "thaw out,"
instead of simply updating or railing against, the knowingness which underlies that achievement.

And yet, I wonder if there is not another dimension to
the Western tradition that goes unnoticed in all this,
namely, the experience of belonging also to a human socio-cultural world that has not been completely subdued
by the metaphysico-scientific impulse and has always retained a kind of underground existence wherever that
impulse did not entirely predominate. It is just this kind of

experience, I think, from which Socrates could still easily take his cue. Hence, when he asks his interlocutors to tell him what they really mean, he expected to hear opinions arising, not from unthawed natural knowingness, but from unrecognized socio-cultural attitudes. That this other dimension has indeed been secondary in Western philosophy seems clear enough. But perhaps there is now the opportunity to recover it out of the dissatisfying ending of that philosophy. And if so, then two things would appear to be necessary. First, assuming my reading of Socrates is basically on target, much more extensive characterizations of his kind of activity are needed in order to bring it fully out from under the shadow of our Platonic heritage. In this, I have proposed, *Time, Space, and Knowledge* speaks directly to us. But second, if it is indeed to be for us a question of making our understanding or knowingness of the human world at least as important as that of the natural, then we need training in "how it feels" or "what it is like" to open it up. And here, perhaps, I might suggest supplementing the meditative exercises in *Time, Space, and Knowledge* with—what else?—dialogues of the Socratic kind.

That these remarks are deliberately formulated in the first person should, of course, be taken very seriously.

Note

1. Tarthang Tulku, *Time, Space, and Knowledge: A New Vision of Reality* (Emeryville, Calif.: Dharma Publishing, 1977).

CHAPTER 2

Kaisa Puhakka's paper "Beyond Outer and Inner Space" is an investigation of unreflective, common-sense philosophy, in terms of which those things farthest from our actual experience are most real, and that which is immediately present is least real. Thus, from a common-sense perspective, objects are more real than ordinary physical space, which, in turn, is more real than awareness.

Dr. Puhakka, however, suggests that common sense has it completely backwards, since awareness is more comprehensive and permanent than physical objects, and that *Time, Space, and Knowledge* offers a means to set the order right again. One path back, in her estimation, begins with extending the concept of physical space to our subjective world and culminates in transcending the inner outer dichotomy by opening to the nonlocated pervasiveness of (nonphysical) space.

Such a reordering has far-reaching consequences. Dr. Puhakka argues, for example, that the psychological issues of freedom vs. determinism and mind vs. body, based on commonsense views about objects, can be opened up, along with these objects, by means of the intellectual analysis and visualization exercises in *Time, Space, and Knowledge*. Moreover, after considering various conventional theories about the mind and the role of (nonphysical) space in displaying mental objects, Dr. Puhakka explores the possibility of moving beyond the mind-self toward a wholly new concept of *person.*

The first section of Dr. Puhakka's article concludes that our commonsense, ordinary level ordering of reality is backwards. The truth of this statement may be seen not by intellectual analysis alone, but by means of a more encompassing and open, second or third level knowledge. Second level 'knowing', included in the term *awareness*, shows 'things', physical space, and the observing self to be interrelated manifestations of 'timing', not independent and impermeable items. Third level knowledge or awareness appreciates things, physical space, and the self as appearances without boundaries of any kind and without even having 'happened'.

For readers interested in exploring the mind-body problem further, we recommend the papers by D. Beere, A. Foster, R. Puligandla, and J. White; further material on alternative orderings of reality may be found in the article by A. Egendorf. Chapters 1–4 of *Time, Space, and Knowledge* will provide helpful background material and experiential exercises on the topics covered in Dr. Puhakka's paper.

Kaisa Puhakka

Beyond Outer and Inner Space

I

When reading Tarthang Tulku's *Time, Space, and Knowledge*, one cannot but be struck by the extraordinary clarity and depth of the vision that emerges from its pages.[1] It does not merely rearrange the furniture of our ordinary knowledge by substituting a new set of assumptions and 'first principles' for old ones; it renders all such assumptions and first principles fluid and transparent. It is a vision as boundless and translucent as the space that it opens up; indeed, no boundary separates it from that space, but the two are one.

Yet, as Tarthang Tulku anticipates in his preface, "Some passages and exercises may seem difficult or opaque at first . . ." (p. xxxiii).* Where does the difficulty and opaqueness come from? The answer seems simple enough: it comes from the same place we do. And where do we

---

*This and all the parenthetical page references that follow are to *Time, Space, and Knowledge.*—ED.

---

come from? This is not so easy to answer as the first question, yet it seems to me important enough to merit consideration. So my reflections on *Time, Space, and Knowledge* begin with what may be called our *common sense*: the basic, gut-level feelings we have about what is "really real," no matter what others may say.

Philosophers, scientists, and men of learning often display contempt toward what they call "common sense," the naive and prejudiced views that unschooled people entertain about themselves and the world. As a consequence, *commonsensical* is considered to be a term applying to certain kinds of views—usually views that differ from those of current scientific and philosophic theories. But we shall understand 'commonsensical' in a more fundamental sense as meaning simply 'unreflective'. In this sense it is not an exclusive prerogative of the layman, but characterizes the attitudes and behaviors of everyone, including the scientist and the philosopher, *almost all the time*. (For the moments of reflection about oneself and the world are rare indeed, even in the library and the laboratory.) In short, when views are considered, not in the timeless abstract, but in their concrete attitudinal and behavioral manifestations over time, then it is fair to say that, most of the time, we are unreflective, commonsense philosophers, regardless of our professional preoccupations.

I shall now venture to make a few observations about some of the most basic features of commonsense philosophy and certain associated psychological attitudes. Common sense is, of course, not unconnected with science and philosophy; quite the contrary, it shapes the foundations of all the academic disciplines to some extent. Yet, there are certain peculiarities of common sense that are not generally shared by the academic disciplines. First, commonsense philosophy differs from academic philosophy in having a very hazy concept of 'reality'. Unlike the academic conceptions, in which something is either real or unreal, the commonsense conception admits degrees of reality. Thus, some things are more real than others. (This is not unlike the commonsense practice of democracy, in which some people are more equal than others—a view not accepted by academic theories of democracy.)

Second, common sense considers those things that are farthest removed from actual experience as the most real, and, conversely, those things that are most immediately and pervasively present are considered least real. Thus, the things that are most real to us are physical objects —trees, rocks, cars, people, and so on. The space between these things seems to be of more dubious reality, in spite of the fact that space is everywhere around us and no part of it could ever disappear (that is, become nonexistent), whereas objects disappear all the time. But there is a sense in which even space, as the medium in which physical objects appear, can be made to disappear along with the objects—by closing one's eyes. The commonsense philosopher in us would immediately object that physical objects and space do not really cease to exist in the process.

However, our point is not to argue about what 'really exists.' It is, rather, to call attention to something that is so pervasive that it does not disappear even for the person who closes his eyes—the awareness that remains quite uninterrupted regardless of whether the *objects* of aware-ness seem to be 'outside' or 'inside' the eyelids. Yet, this awareness seems to have the least reality for us. Thus, we are aware of physical objects all the time, and we some-times get a vague sense of the space between them, but how often are we aware of awareness?

The third point concerning common sense has to do with the psychological attitudes that are intimately con-nected with its concept of reality. For instance, unreal things produce fear in us; or, in terms of the degrees of reality to which common sense subscribes, the less real something is, the more fear it produces in us. We are not in the grip of fear all the time because less real or unreal things are seldom objects of our experience—and that, in turn, is the reason they are not regarded as real in the first place. Thus, for example, most of us do not believe that ghosts are real, and, of course, we do not usually encounter such beings. However, if perchance we did run across one, we would likely be far more frightened than would some-one who believed that they *are* real.

Consider now our common attitudes toward physical objects, space, and awareness. Many people pre-fer to live in relatively crowded conditions and may im-plicitly identify culture and civilization with such condi-tions. Even those who live in the country because they like to have more room would rather avoid a wholly deserted area where there is not much besides open space to look at and be with. Even the few desert and mountaintop "freaks" can seldom endure solitude and open space very long; fewer still would choose such solitude as a permanent way of life. There are, of course, many kinds of reasons for people's preferences concerning their living arrangements: social, political, economic, and so on. But the frequent avoidance of open spaces, and the discomfort that most of us would feel if we were forced to stare into space longer than the daydreams that keep us from attending to it last, suggest a psychological reason as well—fear.

There is something even more disconcerting than being in open spaces—being alone with eyes closed or, even if they are open, seeing only opaque surfaces. Usually one is then dwelling in the inner realm of thoughts, images, and memories. Being in a daydream is not threatening in itself, for while it lasts it is not different from being with physical things and people. Indeed, one usually encounters one's favorite people and things there, in the most exhilarating episodes. What makes daydreams threatening is the fact that we wake up from them, and, upon awakening, the unreality of the dream stares us in the face mockingly. We have been fooled! We prefer to make such encounters with "unreality" as brief and rare as possible: in the midst of dreaming, we do not think of awakening, and when awakening occurs (usually without our intentions having anything to do with it), we forget our dreams remarkably rapidly. We are interested in the contents of our dreams only insofar as we believe that they may have some bearing on our "real life." But dreaming *as dreaming*, apart from its contents, is unreal.

So, too, is thought *as thinking*. The thought of a thought apart from its object is likely to elicit an eerie feeling of sheer nothingness, a bottomless abyss beyond the possibility of imagination, even more threatening than open space, which at least is bounded by objects. Yet, thoughts cannot be thought away, as objects and even the space between them can. Something remains which is not a thing at all, and this something pervades physical objects and space as well.

This last point is important, so let me dwell on it a little longer. What remains when all else is removed from the field of experience is awareness. True enough, we rarely experience awareness, because most of the time we experience what we take to be physical things (trees, skyscrapers, people, and so on). But being an object of experience does not guarantee that the object exists beyond the experience. Common sense, too, distinguishes between being an object of experience and really existing.

So how do we decide whether something genuinely exists? We share our experiences of physical things with other people, and the fact that we can talk about our common experiences gives us the feeling that the objects of such experiences exist independently of our being aware of them. However, this feeling is not the same as actually knowing, but is more like *believing*. And what we *do* know about the objects of such beliefs is that they change and pass away; none of them remains forever. How, then, do we know that awareness exists? The answer is simple: by being aware. This answer, revealed in the very asking of the question, represents the most direct and incontrovertible kind of knowing that there is, in which knowing is the same as *being*. What is more, the answer is always the same, for awareness does not change due to time and circumstances. It always is.

Thus, it seems that common sense has it all backwards. Physical objects—those things whose existence is most precarious and transient, impossible to certify without relying on the testimony of others—we consider to be most real and feel most comfortable with. But that which is all-pervasive and whose existence is beyond doubt— namely, awareness—we consider least real and feel uncomfortable with. We are thus engaged in a self-defeating quest for permanence where none exists, and we are haunted by ghosts that cannot be made to go away.

Only a new vision that reaches to the core of our unreflective common sense could turn such a backward ordering of reality around and allow us to dwell comfortably in a reality that pervades everything. *Time, Space, and Knowledge* offers such a vision. It is a uniquely profound work in that it addresses not just this or that particular theory or position, but examines notions that are so fundamental as to lie at the foundations not only of all scientific and philosophical views, but of common sense as well.

What could be common to all thought and experience? The answer offered by Tarthang Tulku is: time, space, and knowledge. These are universally present in all human thought and experience. It is not that some particular conception of time, space, and knowledge is universal. We know that various theories about them have been proposed by philosophers and scientists in different ages, and we also know that the concept of time and space presupposed by physics has changed with the emergence of relativity theory. But one thing has not changed—the fact that some concept of time and space, whether it be Newtonian absolute time and space, Einsteinian space-time, or something else, lies at the foundation of all experience and knowledge. This can be easily verified by simply asking: Could something that neither occupies space nor endures in time be an object of knowledge for me? Could I even conceive of the existence of such a thing? The answer to each of these questions, directly verifiable in one's experience, is no, *regardless of what one takes the 'thing' or 'space' or 'time' to be.*

We thus start with space and time even before agreeing upon a definition of them; they are there as soon as we experience anything at all. So it becomes possible to conduct an inquiry into space, time, and knowledge, the results of which are not contingent upon an initial acceptance of arbitrary definitions. *Time, Space, and Knowledge* undertakes such an inquiry. Or, since the investigation begins and ends with our experience, including the commonsensical, it may be more correct to say that *Time, Space, and Knowledge* points the way for the reader to undertake the inquiry for himself. And because such an inquiry is grounded in the phenomenology of immediate and, hence, incontrovertible experience, it has the power to effect a profound transformation in the investigator.

The suspicion with which we tend to view all claims of universality is certainly justifiable. The supposedly universal principles usually become abstract, lifeless skeletons to which the variety of concrete experience is reduced, and thereby drained of its lifeblood. But far from being an abstract vanishing point of all experience, space and time are progressively expanded in *Time, Space, and*

Knowledge into a vision that accommodates ever wider variety and new dimensions of experience. Such a vision is the result of a gradual liberation from the ordinary concepts of space and time which, at the foundations of ordinary knowledge, set the limits of our experience. Ordinary space, which at once defines the boundaries of and is bounded by objects, opens up to Great Space where all boundaries are transcended. Similarly, ordinary time which even in its most far-reaching aspect extends only in one direction (and hence remains a tunnel vision) is opened up to Great Time where the separations between 'before', 'now', and 'after' are transcended.

Time, Space, and Knowledge shows that the gaps in ordinary space and the separations in ordinary time are what *constitute* objects in ordinary knowledge (cf. pp. 62, 127, 172–73), and that they also are responsible for the precariousness and transience built into the reality of such objects (cf. pp. 124–28, 137, and 153). But because Great Space and Great Time encompass the time and space of conventional reality, the limitations and transience of such a reality are not abolished but accommodated. From this accommodation arises an understanding and a joyful acceptance of the precariousness, the sorrows, and the sufferings of the world.

II

The remainder of this essay will focus on 'space' as it relates to our efforts to understand ourselves. I shall try to show how, by extending the conventional notion of physical space 'out there' to the subjective realm 'in here' and by finally transcending this dichotomy in an unbroken, all-pervasive vision of Great Space, our understanding also expands progressively toward ever wider perspectives until finally all perspectives, and therewith their built-in problems, are transcended in what Tarthang Tulku calls "Great Knowledge."

According to *Time, Space, and Knowledge,* "Inside or beneath the opacities and hard surfaces which define us and our encounters, there is also space. Intangible, immeasurable psychological spaces constitute the person whose body we see as definite and localized" (p. 3). In thus extending the concept of space to the inner, psychological realm, Tarthang Tulku is already stepping beyond the conventions that govern the sciences and much of philosophy. For conventional knowledge tells us that space is 'out there', not 'in here'. As the eighteenth century philosopher Immanuel Kant said, space is the necessary condition of "outer experience," by which he meant experience of the physical world. For Kant, as for modern scientists and most philosophers, thoughts, feelings, memories, and other subjective events cannot be located anywhere in space, hence such "inner experiences" are said to occur only in time. True, we sometimes talk poetically about the inner spaces of imagination, the 'mindscape'; but few self-respecting psychologists would take such talk to be anything but metaphorical.

In *Time, Space, and Knowledge,* however, 'space' is space, whether it refers to the inner or the outer world. There is no subtle shift in ontological status from 'real' to 'unreal' or even 'less real', as is implied in a move from the literal to the metaphorical understanding of 'space'. The move is made because of our prior commitment to the dichotomies of inner vs. outer, and mental vs. physical. By the same token, a fresh, unprejudiced approach to space *as space* leads to a transcendence of these dichotomies. Of course, seeing space as space in all its manifestations, inner as well as outer, is easier said than done. Indeed, 'saying' does not take us very far at all; the work must be done silently and patiently with one's immediate experience. To this end, *Time, Space, and Knowledge* offers a rare treasure of practical exercises that provide invaluable guidance, strength, and inspiration for the work.

Before the 'inner space' can be explored, then, the obstacles created by the commonsensical assumptions about 'outer space' must be cleared away. These assumptions are manifested in the two most fundamental issues of psychology, namely those of freedom vs. determinism, and mind vs. body. Although these two problems are usually treated as if they are independent of one another, it is not difficult to see that they are tied together logically.

The issue of freedom vs. determinism involves two mutually exclusive conceptions of the human being. The one holds that people are like machines, in that all their actions, thoughts, and feelings are determined by environmental 'fuels' and the 'nuts and bolts' of their biological constitution. The other maintains that people are free and self-determined, that there is a "ghost" in the machine, namely the 'self' that is the true agent of our actions. For most psychologists and philosophers, these two views exhaust all the possibilities, and so one is forced to choose between them.

Since the 'free agent' is not a physical object (if it were, it would be caused by other physical objects or events), it must, according to standard accounts, be mental. Thus, the advocate of freedom is committed to the view that there is a mental reality that cannot be reduced to physical reality, that is, that mind and body are distinct. And determinism is not necessarily incompatible with mentalism, for the mental realm could conceivably be governed by its own kind of causal determinism—a view that was indeed held by psychologists like Wundt and Titchener. However, in contemporary psychology and philosophy, determinism has come to be associated with the so-called mind-body identity theory, according to which all mental phenomena are reducible to physical ones, so that perceptions, feelings, and so on, are only symptoms of neurophysiological events. The problems and shortcomings of each of these views are well-known and need not be elaborated here. Instead, I shall now turn to the notions of 'space' and 'object' that underlie them all.

When we want to understand a discipline, we usually look for the assumptions that it makes about its own subject of investigation (for example, 'mind' or 'behavior' in the case of psychology). But sometimes it is more important to look for the assumptions that a discipline makes about things that fall *outside* the sphere of its own investigation and seem remote from its concerns. For, precisely because they do seem far-removed, such assumptions tend to be accepted uncritically and become the unreflective common sense of the discipline.

It is therefore not surprising that the commonsensical views of space and objects have a far greater influence on psychology than on physics, for only in the latter are these taken up for investigation. In psychology, organisms, including human bodies and their physiological structures, are all treated as very solid, with definite boundaries and spatial locations. The indices of stimuli and responses are similarly definite and locatable; otherwise they would not be quantifiable. Moreover, the concept of solid objects with definite boundaries is built into the principle of determinism—regardless of the complications and ramifications, the 'interactions' and 'feedback loops', that have been added on to the original billiard ball model of determinism. The connection here should be obvious; for something to be causally determined, it must have a definite identity, a location in space. (It is, indeed, the nonidentifiability of an elementary particle in space that has rendered causal determinism inapplicable to distinct particles in physics.)

The investigation of solid objects in physics, however, has led, through the discovery of ever finer structures within structures, to a conception of 'object' that is so subtle as to reveal no solidity at all, but only space within space. Thus, in physics, the dichotomy between solid objects and empty space has come very close to breaking down. It is as if elementary particle physics has been, for its practitioners, a long drawn-out "Giant Body" exercise—an exercise which Tarthang Tulku provides for his readers as a vehicle for transcending the body-space dichotomy.

Tarthang Tulku shows that the physicist's concept of 'object' can not only be taken far beyond where physics leaves it, but that such an expansion of our ideas is a necessary preliminary for understanding ourselves and the problem of determinism. So the reader is invited to examine an 'object', both through a subtle analysis that penetrates the veil of our ordinary, commonsense conceptions of it and through visualization exercises that bring about a new experience of 'object'. The outer surfaces of objects give way to inner structures, opacity to translucency; the boundaries no longer separate objects from, but join them to space. Space is now everywhere, both inside and outside objects; indeed, objects *are* space. Such is the new, expanded, fluid vision of space that emerges when our ordinary "frozen" picture of the world is "thawed" (p. 25).

The new vision bears directly on the principle of causal determinism. (See pp. 32–34 and 55–56.) For the operation of causation, as we have seen, presupposes events with distinct boundaries, the one originating from, or being caused by, the other. And when we think abstractly about classes of events or the universe as a whole, we think that a given class of events must have come from another class of events and that the universe itself must have come from something else.

A reexamination of such habits of thought, in light of the new appreciation of space, shows that neither events nor objects are caused by something nonspacious or outside space. Although there is change all around us, and we describe it as one thing giving rise to another, it all happens 'in space'; nothing comes from or goes into something else. But, Tarthang Tulku points out, even the locution *in space* is misleading, because it suggests that objects are different from and merely reside in space. Rather, all is space, the happening, the patterning of space. (See, e.g., Commentary 6, p. 30.) The space that 'appears' to us has no limits beyond which there is something else that gives rise to the appearances. Thus, the frozen picture of billiard balls pushing each other around in space, or being pushed into space from behind, is 'thawed' into a continuous, limitless expanse of "space projecting space into space" (p. 10).

III

Our unreflective common sense tells us that physical objects with solid, definite boundaries are more real than anything else. But the same common sense also tells us that *we* are different from mere physical objects. Consequently, the suggestion that we might gain insight into ourselves by understanding physical objects sounds preposterous at first. To a psychologist, such a suggestion usually brings visions of crass reductionism—the reduction of psychological phenomena to physical. However, with the solidity of physical objects gone, a crucial difference between the 'physical' and the 'mental' worlds now disappears. The intangible, unbounded space strikes us as "almost nonphysical," and this quality was the reason why our common sense was inclined to grant "less reality" to space than to physical objects. But by reversing our commonsense ordering of the reality of objects and space, Tarthang Tulku prepares the ground for the next step—an opening up to the reality of inner space.

The last obstacle that remains to a fully open, limitless space is the mind. As long as space 'surrounds' without yet entering into the observer, as long as there is an 'in here' from which the 'out there' is surveyed, there remains a gap in space. The 'mind', by which we mean whatever the 'in here' is taken to be, is also opaque, but its opaqueness is far subtler than that of physical objects. For this reason, it is actually more difficult to penetrate mind than physical objects. The opaqueness of physical objects is an undeniable fact that stares one right in the face. So one knows where one stands initially with respect to physical objects. But mind, being more subtle and elusive, can easily be thought of as nonexistent or 'less real,' and both common sense and philosophy provide support for such a view. Yet, its subtle existence may have merely escaped us—only to make itself felt again in common sense, which tells us that we are somehow different from physical objects.

So we do not know very clearly how we stand with respect to the mind, especially if our commonsensical or philosophical predilections lead us to deny its existence. For we do not know exactly what it is whose existence we want to affirm or deny. As a consequence, theories of mind typically do two things at once: they deny the existence of the mind in one sense and affirm it in another, usually more subtle, sense. In contrast to all such approaches, *Time, Space, and Knowledge* invites the reader to investigate in his direct experience what it is whose existence or nonexistence philosophers as well as psychologists are concerned with. (See chapter 3.)

A theory of mind associated with empiricist philosophy and much of contemporary psychology earned its respectability by rejecting the "ghost" in the machine. Introspective investigation revealed no "little man inside the head" producing thoughts, images, and feelings. There was no 'self' viewing the objects of perception, thought, and feeling, but just these objects. Hence 'mind' came to be identified with mental objects and events. Since the 'self' was no longer the source of these objects, the question remained as to what causes the mental objects and events. One contemporary answer is that we do not, and in principle cannot, know; for whatever we do know is itself a mental object and hence in need of an explanation. This is what Tarthang Tulku calls the "self-reference and the 'category' perspective" on the mind (p. 52). By considering mental objects as belonging to a separate, irreducible category, this view renders the mind wholly opaque and mysterious, altogether beyond the possibility of further investigation.

The other contemporary approach mentioned in *Time, Space, and Knowledge* consists of the various mind-body identity theories. These theories seek to establish the source of mental phenomena in the physical realm. But since physical causes can only produce physical effects, it then becomes necessary to view the mental objects themselves as somehow physical. "So [according to this account] it is, in fact, some physical interaction that produces or actually constitutes (in some obscure sense) the psychic experience of the 'investigating self', 'thoughts', and 'a mind having thoughts' " (p. 53).

The phrase *mind-body identity* is thus not altogether appropriate, for rather than being simply concerned with removing the distinction between mind and body, the aim of these theories is to *reduce* mind to body. The trouble is that it does not occur to the proponents of such theories to ask themselves what it is that they are trying to reduce to the physical, or why there is a need for such a reduction in the first place. Thus, the identity theorists are even less inclined than the category theorists to investigate the mental objects as they appear in their immediate experience. They quickly pass from the mental events to mere talk about them, that is, to the "mentalistic vocabulary" which they claim to be translatable to the vocabulary of neurophysiology. They never stop to wonder how the mentalistic vocabulary came to be, if, as they suppose, there are only neurophysiological events to start with.

As Tarthang Tulku observes, "Both of these two conventional perspectives on 'mind' deny the validity of our recourse to immediate experience in searching for the 'mind' " (p. 53). But this seems ironic, for we just noted that contemporary theories of mind are based on the discovery, made by "recourse to immediate experience," that the mind is nothing but the set of mental objects that appear in introspection, or "a bundle or collection of different perceptions" as the British philosopher David Hume described it.[2] Is something missing in the equation which states that the mind equals a set of mental objects? It does seem so. What is missing from the introspective data is the *space* in which the mental objects occur—not another object such as a 'self', but the overall 'happening' of the introspection itself.

Thus, being exclusively concerned with the results of his introspective discovery, Hume was unaware of what was actually happening as the discovery itself was taking place. This probably explains the curious fact that he claimed, on the one hand, to know *how* to "enter most intimately into what I call *myself*"[3] and, on the other hand, denied finding any self there. It did not occur to Hume to inquire how such entrance was accomplished (surely not bodily, as one would enter a room), or what exactly he did enter, if not the self. Similarly, it did not occur to psychologists like Wundt and Titchener, who also employed introspection as a method of investigating the mind, that the act of introspection was itself mental. (Certainly no physical measures or apparatus were involved.) Had this occurred to them, they would have realized that there is more to mind than just a set of objects.

But just as it is initially difficult to realize that physical space is not simply an empty container for solid objects, so, too, it is difficult to see 'beyond' and 'through' mental objects and to realize the continuity of space which displays these objects. The opacity of the mental objects consists of the meanings, symbols, and images which refer to objects and events in the 'outside world' and which also have the power to capture our attention and instantly transport it there. According to Tarthang Tulku, "Meanings cannot show Great Space, precisely because they draw one out, making 'here' dependent for its significance on 'out there', 'up ahead', 'behind and in the past' " (p. 100). No sooner do we engage in thinking than we become engrossed in the objects of thought, meanings, and actually *forget* that we are thinking. This instantaneous forgetfulness makes it very nearly impossible to become aware of thoughts *as thoughts* rather than of the objects of thought, and it is, indeed, one of the basic manifestations of *avidya* ("ignorance") which, ironically enough, is the hallmark of common sense.

It is our forgetfulness that makes daydreams seem so pleasantly and reassuringly real while they last. But the realization that one is engrossed in *objects* of thought all the time, whether dreaming or not, can produce an awakening so powerful as to render our ordinary waking reality not much better or more real than a dream.

But how is such an awakening to be accomplished? There is no way that it could be accomplished by verbal comprehension of verbal truths, for the liberation of awareness from the captivity of words and symbols is precisely what is at issue. It is here that we reach the shore beyond which conceptual analysis cannot carry us. A different kind of vehicle is needed from this point on. Such a vehicle is provided by the exercises in *Time, Space, and Knowledge*, particularly those in which observation is focused on the space between thoughts, and on thoughts themselves as space (exercises 12 and 13). Thus, the reader is asked to observe carefully the arising and passing away of thoughts, which makes it "possible to discover a kind of gap or space between [them]" (p. 58). This may be a beginning of the realization that mind is not a set of objects, that is, images and meanings. And when one then attends to thought *as thought* and meaning *as meaning*, that is, to "the quality of thoughts in their immediate presence," then one may begin to penetrate their opacity and come to clearly see that "thoughts, meanings, and mental events may themselves be the 'space' which is uncluttered by thoughts, and the 'knowing' which is un-deceived by meanings" (p. 61).

With the uncluttering of mind, inner space opens up. But who is viewing this space? Who is the neglected introspectionist in Hume's analysis of mind? The answer is, nobody—or rather, as Tarthang Tulku puts it, "no mind." For space, whether outer or inner, has no limits and hence no 'outside' from which it can be viewed as an object. (See pp. 63–67 and 145.) By limiting 'mind' to its objects, Hume and the introspective psychologists left out the subject, without realizing that there can be no objects without a subject. The two arise together as the two sides of a single dichotomy: that of the inside (subject) and outside (object). This dichotomy may have, itself, been turned inside out by Hume and the later psychologists, since they claimed to be investigating the 'inside' of their own minds, but always left themselves 'outside' such investigations. The point is that whether the subject is thought to be inside or outside, it must always be on the opposite side of the object. This is because "this mind-self lacks a sufficiently wide perspective to take itself into account, and its status as an apparently *independent and potent entity depends on that very limitation*" (p. 67). Having transcended this limitation, one may at last see that, indeed, "there are no gaps" (p. 67); the inner is not distinct from the outer; there is just space, Great Space.

IV

We may finally ask, what is the understanding of *person* that emerges from the vision of Great Space? Ordinarily, we know ourselves to be bound to solid bodies and fixed patterns of behavior; our responses to the present are conditioned by past experience and perhaps even genetic constitution. But we also feel that it is within our power to break the habitual ways of thinking and acting (although it must be admitted that, being caught in the rut of daily routine, we seldom actually exercise such power and seldom even remember having it). As if to account for the patterns of human behavior which are not yet wholly frozen, but contain an element of unpredictability, most conventional psychologists would agree on a minimal definition of 'person' as a 'set of *tendencies* to behave in certain ways'. In *Time, Space, and Knowledge* the word *tendency* is also used:

> ... the 'person in a world' could more accurately be seen as a *tendency* toward consolidation or birth in (or as) what for that world are successive moments. The 'person' is then a summary notion describing the overall *attempt* to set up a frozen pattern or series of instants connected in an exclusive manner, in contrast to a more open and inclusive 'space'. (p. 33)

There is, however, a profound difference between the understanding of *tendency* expressed in the passage above and that found in conventional psychology. In conventional psychology, the behavioral tendencies that constitute personality are determined by past learning and genetic constitution, the frozen patterns and solid objects of the world. In *Time, Space, and Knowledge*, however, the tendency is *fundamental* and not determined by something else; there is nothing frozen or solid, only a tendency toward freezing. The view of 'person' as the tendency to form habits and establish routines, rather than as behavioral tendencies determined by previously established habits and routines, also accommodates the humanistic perspective of freedom, without indulging in the easy optimism of believing in a self that "freely chooses" the habits and patterns of behavior.

It might be tempting to consider the openness of space as the source of freedom, as a sort of expanded self, perhaps. However, such a view commits the subtle error of reifying the dichotomy of space vs. the tendency to freeze into patterns. Rather: "No 'freezing' or anomalous tendency has set itself up in contrast to 'space'. The frozen pattern is neither frozen nor even a 'freezing'. Worlds, things, and persons remain 'space' rather than only deriving from 'space' . . . " (p. 34).

Thus, when we let go of the ignorance that we glorify as common sense, we begin to see that everything remains as it is. And when the inner space of things and, finally, of ourselves opens up, then we see that everything not only is, but always has been and always will be as it is. Space accommodates all, even our commonsense world, and we have lost nothing. But by reversing the commonsense ordering of reality we have gained everything: the continuity that permeates the separateness of our existence and the eternity that looms in the transience of our lives.

Notes

1. Tarthang Tulku, *Time, Space, and Knowledge: A New Vision of Reality* (Emeryville, Calif.: Dharma Publishing, 1977).

2. David Hume, *Hume Selections*, ed. C. W. Hendel, Jr. (New York: Charles Scribner's Sons, 1955), p. 85.

3. Ibid., p. 84.

CHAPTER 3

Psychotherapy has helped many people deal with the various kinds of chronic psychological "stuckness" that are generally termed *neuroses*. But frequently, as Bill Jackson points out, the success of standard approaches is partial at best. A patient's dominant neurotic symptoms may disappear only to be replaced by others that are equally debilitating. Or again, lifelong conflicts may be resolved without the patient's experiencing an improvement in the overall quality of his or her life. And what does a therapist do for someone who is, by all the usual standards, well adjusted and successful, but who nevertheless finds life stale and meaningless?

Dr. Jackson suggests that occurrences such as these betray the limits of therapies that focus on specific symptoms and their causes, and that consider a patient cured when his or her behavior and self-image are brought within the bounds of 'normalcy'. What is called for, in his estimation, is a broadening of perspectives and a recognition that something more fundamental is at issue.

Because of the penetrating intellectual and experiential analysis of 'self' and 'world' in *Time, Space, and Knowledge*, Dr. Jackson believes that it offers a "viable step beyond psychotherapy." The book not only shows how conflict and frustration derive from the preoccupation with boundaries that characterizes the ordinary world-view, it also provides the means for 'seeing through' these partitions. Then ordinary knowledge, which by its nature involves a deadening repetitiousness and the maintenance of rather rigid 'positions', can make way for a 'knowingness' that 'sees' all appearances as the naturally healthy play of space and time. No longer "bottoming out" on 'things'—subjects and objects—one finds that tendencies to get and remain "stuck" dissolve of their own accord, and so taking care of oneself becomes a real possibility.

The Foreword to this anthology, along with chapters 1, 2, 4, 6, 9, 10, and 14 of *Time, Space, and Knowledge*, will provide some useful background material, and for those interested in other perspectives on the Time-Space-Knowledge vision and psychology, we recommend the articles by A. Egendorf, R. Puligandla, and R. Romanyshyn.

Bill Jackson

Psychological Growth
in and beyond Psychotherapy

Tarthang Tulku makes a succinct and wholly valid
statement in *Time, Space, and Knowledge*:[1]

> We have limitless possibilities to find fulfillment and satis-
> faction in our lives and in our relationships with one an-
> other. By learning to directly contact the essence of our
> being, we can discover an unbounded freedom which is not
> only a freedom from some external restraint, but is itself the
> dynamic expression of the meaning and value of being
> human. Once this intrinsic freedom becomes a lived reality,
> then all other freedoms naturally follow. (p. xxxv)*

While this statement may seem clear enough to those of us
who were born with an intuitive self-awareness or who,
through long and arduous scholarship and self-discipline,
have attained it to a degree, there are many people in the
world to whom such a statement would make no sense at
all. To these people, who certainly constitute the majority
of mankind, it would sound, at best, like an idealistic

---

*This and all of the parenthetical page references that follow are to
Time, Space, and Knowledge.—ED.

© Copyright 1980 Dharma Publishing. No part of this article may be reproduced in any
form without written permission from Dharma Publishing, 2425 Hillside Avenue,
Berkeley CA 94704.

promise of something which they themselves could never attain. They are simply too caught up in their own (samsarically) conditioned distractions, conflicts, and anxieties to take seriously the possibility that the comprehension and contemplation of *Time, Space, and Knowledge* may offer them a way out of these very dilemmas. A man occupied with both hands full of rattlesnakes is reluctant to reach for the rope which might pull him out of the snake pit.

Within the range of human experience, perhaps the point farthest away from enlightenment is that psychological state which we describe as neurotic. The neurotic is so utterly preoccupied with his own moment-to-moment conscious and unconscious feelings and conflicts, and with what seems to be a constantly threatening world around him, that he can never (in an almost literal psychological sense) see beyond the tip of his own nose. His perception of life is diametrically opposite to that seen by the liberated mind. He is isolated and largely helpless in a hostile world, where he is constantly threatened and must make huge efforts to cope and survive. Otherwise, he might be at any moment overwhelmed and destroyed.

While this constant and intense struggle may go on largely at unconscious levels and be expressed overtly only through symptoms, it is, in a general sense, the psychodynamic picture of all neurotics. Yet, as has been empirically demonstrated in any number of clinical cases with which I have worked, this apparently helpless and hopeless neurotic can also attain the vision and experience of freedom described by Tarthang Tulku in *Time, Space, and Knowledge*. It is simply a longer trip for some of us than for others.

One must, of course, be very careful not to oversimplify in equating a dimension of 'ignorance-enlightenment' with a dimension of 'neurosis-psychological health'. Still, a path toward psychological wellness can be postulated, leading from repression, ignorance, and egocentrism toward awareness, enlightenment, and egolessness. Clearly, such a path must at some point pass out of the domain of scientific psychology and clinical psychotherapy, and cross the vague boundaries that separate them from philosophy, theology, and cosmology.

I have traveled only a small portion of this path myself, but I have known many others who have traveled other parts. By drawing upon all of our experiences, I will be able to describe this psychic sojourn, at least in general terms. The scenery is made up of the people whom one finds at various points along the pathway. Their characteristics typify them and make them recognizable as being at a particular point in their own expedition toward liberation. As in any travelogue, even one of the mind, there are some who have found more direct paths, many who have wandered over much more serpentine, devious routes, and any number who have taken sideroads into different realms altogether. Nevertheless, we can describe general directions and landmarks which may be helpful in establishing our state of progress and in orienting us toward the goal of liberation.

Neurosis as a Shrinking World

O ne thing can be said about the neurotic that will not require our becoming enmeshed in the numerous, complex, and contradictory behavioral and dynamic theories of neurosis: he is, in many ways, a child who psychologically never grew up. It is a widespread misconception that because children have, in some ways, a less intellectualized, more direct awareness of themselves and their world, they are therefore closer than the adult to a state of transcendent self-liberation. Evans-Wentz contributes to this wrong thinking when he writes, "As study of the mind of children shows, there is a natural inborn tendency in man to transcend the external world of nonhomogeneity and to seek a state of homogeneity, such as that of the supra-mundane at-one-ment which results from the Yogic knowing of the mind in its unobscured naturalness."[2] While there is a certain tangential validity in that statement, he then goes on to conclude that "there have been no more profound psychologists than the Great Teachers, who, with unanimity, have proclaimed that the Neophyte must become as a little child before he can enter into the Realm of Truth."[3] And he puts the torch of immortalization to this pyre of illogic by concluding that "the wisdom of babes is greater than that of scholars."

The fact is that while young children do have a somewhat direct perception of reality, unobscured by intellectual abstraction, they are, at least at a conscious level, in a psychic state that is diametrically opposite to that of the liberated sage. The young child's orientation is highly egocentric; he sees himself as the center of the world.

The sage, in contrast, has reached a state of egolessness and has surrendered his narcissistic self to the transcendent Self or Mind. The process of growing up is largely a progression of successive stages of projection, identification, and transference to the people and world outside of oneself. And one would be tempted to say, from a psychological viewpoint, that Hinduism and Buddhism represent the ultimate point of identification outside of oneself, where virtually no psychic energy remains invested in the egoistic self. It is easy to see, then, that when one says that the neurotic is still trapped in the egocentrism of the child, it is not at all a good thing. People whose development has been arrested at this stage, without the elaboration of further, more specific, neurotic syndromes, are characterized by selfishness, narcissism, a lack of empathy, and an excessive pleasure drive.

But the person who becomes genuinely stuck at this early childhood level of egocentrism actually begins moving backwards psychologically. His ego-bound stance in life comes more and more into opposition with the responsible, caring, giving, and sharing world of the mature adult, so that, on the one hand, he is increasingly unwilling and unable to meet the social expectations of the world around him, and on the other, he becomes increasingly frustrated as his narcissistic demand that the world be as he wishes it to be is not met. He is driven more and more, in reaction to this, into an obsession with his own isolated self. He may eventually find himself so at odds with and isolated from the world around him that this self-encased self-obsession becomes a chronic conscious experience of depersonalization. He may spend most of his time preoccupied with his situation, while simultaneously feeling that the world, other people, and even he himself are somehow not real. In contrast to Tarthang Tulku's exercise of learning to experience the "Giant Body," he has psychically shrunk to a single point.

As the neurotic begins to feel more isolated in his own self-obsession, the world, too, begins to fill this psychological void and seems to close in more and more, until he may begin to experience intense anxieties and fears. These may take the form of focused phobias, obsessive-compulsive anxieties, or simply vague, chronic feelings of impending doom. And it is only natural, given his egoistic and samsaric orientation, that he should begin searching for the 'something' which is causing the intense feelings of frustration and anger, anxiety and fear, depression and loneliness.

If these sorts of events take place primarily at a conscious level, but the person continues to be unable to see any way out of his dilemma, he may eventually reach a kind of existential vacuum in which feelings of futility and meaninglessness set in. On the other hand, if much of this psychological struggle has gone on at an unconscious level, we may see increasing energies put into psychological defenses and the progressive development of clinical symptoms. By the time such defenses and symptoms become apparent, they may have taken on any of the very diverse forms described in the psychiatric and clinical psychological literature, in some cases seeming to be quite bizarre, specific, and detached from the underlying, original 'ego-trappedness' of the individual. If he seeks professional help at this point, he will clearly be perceived as having a psychological or psychiatric problem; but it is likely to be misperceived, by an equally samsarically oriented professional, as a fear or anxiety related to 'this' or 'that', or a conflict between 'this' and 'that'.

This is not to say that many psychological problems do not have their origins in specific conditioning contingencies, definable psychological conflicts, difficulties in relationships, frustrations in achieving particular goals and need fulfillments, or even in unresolved traumas from earlier life. But it is surprising how often the resolution of these specific problems seems to do little by way of improving the patient's real, general adjustment to life. Genuine meaningfulness or happiness somehow remains elusive. I have personally treated any number of people for whom I cured the particular phobia, resolved the particular conflict, brought to consciousness and dissipated the particular early trauma, or in some other way actually did away with the symptoms, only to have them either return later with some other, new symptom, or else terminate treatment with "maximum benefit," but without really having improved the overall quality of their experience of life. They should have been feeling optimistic and positive about themselves at that point, and they did not. This has led me to conclude that there must be something more deeply, basically, and pervasively wrong with these persons' psyches than the kinds of problems described by Freud, Eysenck, or even Carl Jung.

Of course, there is a general awareness among psychiatrists and psychologists of this 'cure without cure', and every theoretical orientation has its own explanation. The psychoanalysts might conclude that the "underlying neurotic conflict" had not been adequately dealt with; the learning theorists might conclude that some verbal chaining, learning set, or other cognitively conditioned response chains remained; and the eclectic psychiatrists might simply label the patient as "chronic" and leave it at that. But one need not enter this intellectual battlefield to point out that all theories of neurosis and all explanations of treatment outcome revolve around the individual's struggle with himself at a basic level—in other words, with his own ego-boundness. And this is the crucial point, of course: the neurotic is a person who is even more than usually trapped in his individual ego and in the illusion of the desperate reality of the world around him. It is this samsaric illusion in its heightened, acute form which seems, almost by definition, to constitute the prime prerequisite factor in all neuroses. Put conversely, without egoism there can be no neurosis.

Conventional Psychotherapy

The main thrust of the previous discussion was that when the normal, healthy course of psychological growth and development gets "stuck," it does not usually result in a simple cessation of further growth or in some kind of psychological retardation of the developing human psyche; rather, it sets in motion a reverse process of personal involution. The person's world begins to shrink, close in, and bear down upon him, sometimes even crushing him psychically. So, psychoneurosis is a process equally as active and dynamic as the expanding and healthy, ever-increasing growth of consciousness described by Tarthang Tulku—but counter to it. If one thinks of the vision and goal of consciousness described in *Time, Space, and Knowledge* as 'good', then psychoneurosis becomes the epitome of 'evil'. But this is a dualistic way of thinking which we will not pursue further.

Psychotherapy, then, viewed from this perspective, becomes a technique for "unsticking" the person and allowing his psychological and more broadly defined psychic growth to continue. The point of "stuckness" may, for example, actually lie in the person's history of learning and experience, and this is the type of problem to which psychoanalysis addresses itself.

Consider, for example, the case of a girl we may call Carol, with whom I once worked over a long period of time in a psychiatric hospital setting. Carol was attractive, highly intelligent, and when functioning normally, a very nice person. But she went through recurrent periods of acute psychotic disturbance during which she seemed dominated by feelings and conflicts within her own mind, at which times she behaved as though she were truly possessed by demons, and did very destructive things to herself and to others.

Ultimately, through regressive hypnosis we were able to take Carol back to the point in her life at which she had had a very traumatic sexual encounter with her father, and to bring this psychologically paralyzing experience to consciousness. Almost miraculously, once this intense trauma was brought out into the light of her own self-awareness and dissipated, she rapidly recovered, and several years later she sent me a long letter telling me that she had remained happy and had continued in good mental health.

But the case in which one can trace this "stuckness" back to a single traumatic event is unusual. More commonly, thinking and 'self talk' become slightly aberrant and gradually, over a period of years, begin to affect the person's total perception of himself and his world in an increasingly constrictive and, finally, pathological way. (This type of problem, involving the crucial pivot of the ways in which we talk to ourselves within our own minds and the ways we interpret our world in words and other symbols, is addressed by Albert Ellis's Rational-Behavioral Therapy.[4]

An example of this is a patient whom we may call Randolph. From the time he was a very small child, Randolph was constantly taught that the world around him was a dangerous, threatening place with ominous catastrophes ready to befall one at any moment. He heard, for example: "Don't go out without your raincoat and umbrella, or you'll get pneumonia and die"; "If you get poor grades, you'll flunk out of school and be a bum"; "She may seem like a nice girl, but she'll get pregnant and ruin your whole life"; "Being less than the best is failure"; and so on. He began, more and more, to incorporate such messages into his 'self talk'.

Finally, after leading what seemed to be a fairly happy childhood, going on to successfully complete college, marrying a lovely lady, and pursuing a successful career, Randolph's pathologically "stuck" thinking caught up with him. When I saw him, he was in a state of acute depression and anxiety, expressing such irrational fears as these: "Sooner or later my professional colleagues are going to find out that I'm not really competent"; "My wife says she loves me but I just know she's going to leave me"; "The new, expensive house I just bought has something terribly wrong with it"; and so on. After approximately a year of Rational-Behavioral Therapy, Randolph began to get his 'self talk' "unstuck," and his total perception of himself and his world could again begin growing in a more fluid, expanding way.

Still another, even more subtle type of psychological "stuckness" is reflected in the negative self-concept which many people develop as they grow up, or at least biologically mature. This is often not even as specific as negative thoughts or perceptions about oneself or one's world, but is more a general 'state of being' in which the person's experiential world is permeated by a psychological negativity. This is exemplified by a therapy patient whom we may call Mary. The first several months of therapy were quite frustrating in that there seemed to be nothing in particular wrong with Mary's life, intrapsychically or externally. She simply suffered from a vague, amorphous, low-key depression. Slowly, feelings and vaguely expressed perceptions began to surface, indicating that she was somehow unable to be totally herself. After therapy that involved using Carl Rogers's "nondirective" approach, including his general attitude toward the individual, Mary was gradually able to perceive herself as being genuinely "okay" and to begin living in terms of being more freely and totally herself.[5]

Nowadays one often sees people in psychotherapy who do not, superficially, seem to be "stuck" at all and who are, in fact, leading very effective and successful lives, at least in materialistic terms. But these people often present themselves as having a vague but growing feeling of dissatisfaction and emptiness in their lives, as though they are no longer quite sure why they are, still energetically doing the very things in life which they set out to do in the first place. One psychological authority calls it *existential neurosis*, "a relatively new form being described by an increasing number of clinicians. This neurosis is characterized by an intense sense of emptiness and lack of fulfillment in life, even though the afflicted individual may have a well-paying job and be performing effectively in society with regard to material standards."[6]

A particularly striking case of a therapy patient fitting into this type of "stuckness" is that of a man we may call Aaron. Aaron had been an outstanding athlete in college, and he finished school Phi Beta Kappa. He very quickly established himself as professionally capable and became independently wealthy. At the age of thirty, Aaron had a lovely wife and fine children, a beautiful house on the lake in the finest part of town, and drove a superb European sedan. In presenting the problem to me he said, "Here I am approaching thirty-one. I have achieved more than most men and have more money than my grandchildren can spend. So what?"

My own experience, as well as reports from psychotherapists generally, indicates that this type of problem is becoming increasingly common. While not all of those affected are as materially and culturally successful as

Aaron, none seem to have any great problems in their lives, either in terms of the classical neurotic syndromes or in terms of achieving what they currently want in their lives. But they all present this same puzzling question: So what?

It is apparent to me, if not to all psychologists, psychiatrists, and other psychotherapists, that in cases such as Aaron's we are reaching the limits of those techniques, theories, and conceptualizations which conventionally define psychotherapy. There is a dilemma for the therapist confronted with a person who insists, despite his seemingly adequate psychological functions and, conversely, despite the lack of any clearly focused psychological disorder, that he is unhappy and needs help in understanding and living his life. But perhaps this dilemma has always existed and is simply becoming more visible now, as we begin to think in terms of the 'wellness' of one's life as a total growing process, and of all life and existence as somehow interrelated. According to the old ways of thinking (particularly psychiatric thinking as it arose from physical medicine), the assumption was that if one was not 'sick', one was 'well', and that 'curing illness' was all that should be expected. But now a new and pressing question is occurring to many, many people: Well for what?

A Continuously Expanding Awareness

I have discussed psychological living and experience as a process of growth paralleling biological growth. But there is a crucial distinction setting psychological growth apart, and that is the fact that it does not seem to depend, in the last analysis, upon material existence. The implications of this are immense in two ways. First, the process of psychological growth seems potentially to have almost no limits, at least from the human perspective. Second, the dynamic quality of psychological growth is not bound by any material, static conditions, so that if it is not, so to speak, growing in one direction, it will spontaneously begin shrinking in the other direction. Thus psychoneurosis is not simply a process of arrested psychological growth, but one of diminution and shrinking of one's experiential world and self.

Conventional psychotherapy has made great progress over the past century in helping persons to become psychologically "unstuck," but it seems to have fallen into its own kind of "stuckness" by arbitrarily defining its boundary as that point where the patient is simply "unstuck." It is like the situation of finding someone whose cart has bogged down in the mud and stopping, with the best intentions, to help him pull it out—then just riding off without thinking to inquire whether he now knows where he is and where he is going! The underlying nature of this "stuckness" in the psychotherapist himself may lie in the fact that he, as a highly conditioned member of Western society, assumes that the patient, once able to function with basic adequacy, will automatically go about pursuing the culturally defined goals and find happiness. But as Tarthang Tulku points out, "The search for Being is not one which can be based on egoistic purposes and values. Our being has a primordial value that is continuously being worked out within its sphere, and our fulfillment requires that we attend to this value" (p. 296).

This statement is profound in its ramifications for psychotherapy and psychological growth generally. It has implications, in fact, which not only go beyond psychotherapy, but are diametrically opposed to the Western notion of the 'mentally healthy' person as the autonomous and self (ego)-directed individual. And yet, we are becoming acutely aware that this very ego-boundness, as so dramatically illustrated by the aforementioned existential neurosis, is increasingly becoming the felt problem and source of anxiety and unhappiness in many people. Perhaps we need to reformulate the concept of ego itself and to view it as a kind of 'psychic egg' which a person must grow in to a certain point and then break out of, in order that he may continue to develop and expand on a new, higher level of awareness.

The ideas presented here are not really new ones. Especially since World War II, Western thinkers have paid increasing attention to the importance of breaking out of individual, ego-bound consciousness. This was perhaps first recognized by certain members of the existentialist movement, when they sought to elucidate the phenomenon of ego-boundness. Since then, several thinkers have tried to find some way to translate Buddhist and other Eastern thought into usable, meaningful approaches to life for Westerners. Alan Watts made a heroic effort in this direction,[7] and the Transcendental Meditation movement is another such approach. But as a Hindu yogi friend of mine once wryly commented, "Such things are but a single step in a journey of a thousand miles." Moreover, besides this problem of scope, there is the fact that, to date, the interpretations of Eastern philosophies and cosmologies, and the few efforts at translating these views into action, have not been very successful in terms of fitting into our Western ways of thinking and being.

Nevertheless, there are elements of Western philosophical and psychological thinking which do meet, at certain points, with the Eastern, and especially the Buddhist, perspective. For example, Meister Eckhart, the great thirteenth-century Christian mystic, often expresses ideas so close to Eastern thought that he is not infrequently quoted in writings on Buddhism, particularly Zen.[8] And I cannot resist at least mentioning my own little book *Afire with Serenity*, which was written more from intuition than from scholarship, and which attempts to help non-intellectually oriented people attain a degree of ego-transcendence and experience life more directly.[9] But these sorts of writings are parallels, not identities.

The unique gift which Tarthang Tulku has brought us is a *way of doing it.* He has the genius of seeming to understand the Western mentality and being able to present a vision of Being that we can grasp from our own conditioned view of ourselves and our lives. In such books as *Time, Space, and Knowledge* and *Gesture of Balance,*[10] Tarthang Tulku presents what the "Harvard psychologists" might almost consider to be a programmed text in which ideas, exercises, and awareness are presented in a slow, easy progression toward "Wonderment." He has, more than any other living 'guru', in or outside of psychology, presented us with a substantial, valid, and viable step beyond psychotherapy. If psychotherapy can help people become "unstuck," the *Time, Space, and Knowledge* vision gives them wings.

Notes

1. Tarthang Tulku, *Time, Space, and Knowledge: A New Vision of Reality* (Emeryville, Calif.: Dharma Publishing, 1977).

2. W. y. Evans-Wentz, *The Tibetan Book of the Great Liberation* (Oxford: Oxford University Press, 1968), p. 78.

3. Ibid., p. 79.

4. Albert Ellis and Robert Harper, *A New Guide to Rational Living* (North Hollywood: Wilshire Book Co., 1976).

5. Carl Rogers's "nondirective" therapy is succinctly described in T. W. Wann, *Behaviorism and Phenomenology* (Chicago: University of Chicago Press, 1964), pp. 109–40.

6. Frederick Mears and Robert J. Gatchel, *Fundamentals of Abnormal Psychology* (Chicago: Rand McNally, 1979), p. 100.

7. Alan Watts, *Psychotherapy East and West* (New York: Pantheon Books, 1961).

8. See, for example, C. F. Kelley, *Meister Eckhart on Divine Knowledge* (New Haven: Yale University Press, 1977).

9. Bill Jackson, *Afire with Serenity* (Center City, Minn.: Hazelden, 1977).

10. Tarthang Tulku, *Gesture of Balance* (Emeryville, Calif.: Dharma Publishing, 1977).

CHAPTER 4

Edward Casey suggests that our fundamental consciousness of time may be "wholly the work of imagination and memory." So it should come as no surprise that he takes issue with those philosophers who have subordinated imagination and memory to sensation and thought. Such an evaluation, Dr. Casey believes, is grounded in views that ignore certain essential features of experience.

We may, for example, forget that imagination and memory do not always point unequivocally to future and past. The former ranges over *all* possibilities—even those that are connected with no point in 'real' time. Moreover, it is frequently difficult to tell the extent to which a memory is actually a *projection* of what might have been, rather than being simply a recollection of some occurrence.

Such ambiguities and asymmetries seem to allow for forms of temporality in which imagination and memory function in uncommon ways. (Dr. Casey discusses the case of mythic time as an example.) And these, in turn, point to a more basic sort of time that activates the various temporal 'orders' that we either do or might use and live in.

This is Great Time, the dynamic aspect of Being that conveys the unqualified openness of Great Space by exhibiting infinite variety. Yet, so long as the evocations of space are judged by a restrictive knowing to be 'things', time must conform to a linear, 'one at a time' view. Then, since time's messages (including 'memories' and 'imaginings') must assume significance within this context, they are 'flattened out' and robbed of their vitality.

Breathing life back into imagination and memory does not, however, require 'breaking free' of ordinary time. Time binds no one and nothing. The dynamic, inspirational quality of Great Time is 'available' within and *as* ordinary time. Gaining access to it is a matter of opening, and this can begin with a critical investigation of experienced temporality, like the one offered here by Dr. Casey.

Further information about Great Time and ordinary time may be found in Part Two of *Time, Space, and Knowledge,* as well as in this anthology's "Opening Time" and "Orientation to Time, Space, and Knowledge."

Edward S. Casey

Time out of Mind

Philosophical thinking is . . . far less a discovery than a recognition, a remembering, a return, and a homecoming to a remote, primordial, and inclusive household of the soul.
—Friedrich Nietzsche,
Beyond Good and Evil

I

As if anticipating Jungian typologies, Western philosophers have often espoused a fourfold classification of mental activities or faculties. Although the exact constitution of this *quadrivium* of mind differs from philosopher to philosopher, there is a marked tendency from Aristotle onwards to focus on four crucial members: thought (in its various guises as intellect, reason, understanding, etc.); perception (sensation, sensory experience of various kinds); imagination (entertaining mental images, projecting the possible); and memory (retention, recollection, recall). Why these four? Beyond their sweepingly synoptic character when taken together, the four activities in question have the economic advantage of forming two pairs of terms, in each of which there is a compensatory or reciprocal relationship. Thus *thought* and *perception* fall together insofar as what perception gives (i.e., concrete sensory "data") thought lacks, and what thought supplies (i.e., categories, concepts) perception does not possess: "thoughts without [sensory] contents are empty, intuitions without concepts are blind" (Kant, *Critique of Pure Reason*, B 76). Similarly, *imagination* and *memory* belong together by virtue of the fact that memory looks backward toward what has been, while imagination looks forward toward what might be. Such retrospection and prospection complement each other by their very disparateness of directionality.

Philosophers have stressed the importance of the first pair of terms in the context of strictly epistemological questions (the paradigmatic case is that of Kant), whereas the second dyad is singled out in the pursuit of pure description or phenomenology (the paradigm here is Husserl). But we may bring the two pairs together by considering them as forming perpendicular axes in the following fashion:

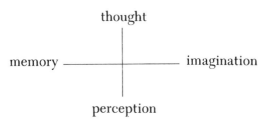

What this simple schema brings to awareness—an awareness which is no less certain for being almost wholly intuitive—is the way in which the two pairs of acts in question relate to the dual dimensionality of *temporality*

or time-as-experienced by human beings. First, the vertical axis unequivocally signifies the *synchronic* dimension of temporality—especially as this is exemplified by the instant or by eternity, neither of which develops or endures in time.[1] Perception tends to take place instantaneously: it apprehends what is *now* present to the senses and is often confined, by the logic of "local partitioning," to this now-point as a "restrictive focal setting."[2] Thought, in contrast yet equally synchronically, ranges over *all* time, time-as-a-whole, and aims at what is *forever* true: its objects are "omnitemporal" in Husserl's term, "eternal" in Plato's. But it is Plato who also tells us that time itself is to be conceived as "the *moving image* of eternity" (*Timaeus* 37d).

Second, the horizontal axis of memory and imagination is the axis of *diachronic* development. On this axis, movement proceeds by images—remembered images retrieving the ever receding antipode of the past, imagined images (or better, imagin*ing* images) leading forward into the future. Beyond this past-future bipolarity, there is a further meaning of the horizontal line: it symbolizes a *fall* into time from the aether of pure thought. The lateral axis is the fallen axis; it is diachronically diffuse; here objects or events falter, linger, and languish.[3]

The foregoing axial opposition may also be thought of in archetypal terms: the erect Apollonic-heroic vertical axis always resisting collapse into the Dionysian dispersion of the horizontal.[4] The temporal dis-tension of the horizontal sweep of time reflects the dismemberment of Dionysus. And, just as Dionysus is re-membered annually, so the time line becomes a ring, an *annulus*, when we recollect a past event which, unrecalled, sinks into shapelessness. A second ring is formed by the anticipation of the future in imagination: imagining projects the future as pure possibility. It is in this double circularization of temporality that the linearity of the horizontal axis (the 'time line') is overcome[5] and that Dionysian recumbency is transformed into the creative cycles of *Rausch*.[6]

II

It is a signal fact, worthy of much wonder, that Western philosophers have (a) assimilated imagining and remembering to each other and even considered them to be the *same* act (for Hobbes, "Imagination and Memory are but one thing, which for divers considerations hath divers names")[7]; and (b) consistently demoted the importance of the two acts, considering each to be inferior or secondary to thought and perception. The latter are typically regarded as *origins* or *sources* of experience and knowledge in contrast with the derivative, nonoriginal character of imagining and remembering. It is not surprising, then, that imagination and memory seem to belong so naturally to a fallen horizontal order of time in which their demoted status is made manifest. Precisely as retrospective and prospective respectively, remembering and imagining exist and exfoliate wholly *within* time, wherein, as children of Chronos, they are devoured at birth by their own progenitor.

In philosophers' eyes, to be thus subject to the ravages of time is to be of lesser value than to be above, beyond, or even beneath time: time's winged chariot is a chariot of

devastation and dis-grace. At the same time, to be a crea-
ture of time is to be difficult to distinguish from *other* fallen
temporal acts and entities; *diacrisis* is rendered problem-
atic by diachrony, whose distendedness creates a continuum of poorly differentiated *temporalia*. The result is
that temporally bound acts such as imagining and remembering, situated as they are on this kind of continuum,
are quickly assimilated to each other; their differences are
reduced to eifferences of degree or nuance only:

> This *decaying sense*, when wee would express the thing it
> self, (I mean *fancy* it selfe,) wee call *Imagination*. . . . But
> when we would express the *decay*, and signifie that the
> Sense is fading, old, and past, it is called *Memory*.[8]

Although memory concerns what is fading and old,
even imagination is in Hobbes's view a form of decay, of
decomposition; both are conceived as mere remnants, *rev-
enants*, of sensation, the only undecayed form of human
experience. Sensation itself exists in a pristine, privileged
state precisely because it takes place *in the instant:* there is
no time for decay in a present moment that is by definition
ever fresh and new. Here the winged chariot appears and
disappears so rapidly that it cannot even begin to be late,
out-of-date, or deteriorated. Chronos does not have time
to devour his own children, for they have not yet even
been brought forth from his own engendering.

Yet we must ask: Does this do justice to imagining and
remembering? Do they simply sit aslant consciousness as
limp, lateral acts? Are they of wholly horizontal significance? Are they to be merged with each other—and then
sacrificed to the maw of thought or perception? Certainly

not. This is not the place to rehearse arguments for the eidetic distinctness of the two acts, or for their nonderivativeness from perception.[9] Nor is it the occasion to argue for the autonomy of imagination—for its unique freedom of mind, which has no parallel in other mental activities.[10] Instead, I shall restrict myself to two points, each unacceptable to mainstream Western thinking: the conjointly crucial (the literally *diacritical*) role of the two acts in the constitution of time-consciousness, and the deeper significance of these acts insofar as they exceed the confines of the everyday awareness of time.

III

Imagining and remembering undeniably have to do with, even if not *only* with, time. Indeed, they are co-essential—which is to say, equally and simultaneously essential—to the human experience of temporality. This can be seen most readily if we adopt the model of time-consciousness proposed by Husserl in his *Phenomenology of Internal Time-Consciousness*.[11] On this model, time-consciousness consists of five phases: the now-point or the present *per se*, the "retention" of the immediate past, the recollection or "secondary remembrance" of the more remote past, the "protention" of the immediate future, and the "anticipation" of the more remote future.

Husserl credits memory (as retentive and recollective) with the constitution of our experience of the past. Yet he fails to specify that it is by *imagining* that our protending and anticipating of the future takes place. Of all mental acts, imagining alone is capable of projecting the future as a region of incompletion and pure possibility. Where memory concerns itself with events as already complete and thus as having what Husserl calls "the unity of the remembered," imagination moves us into the indefiniteness of the *not yet*, of what *might be*.[12] The closed, chthonian character of the one contrasts with the open-ended, aethereal nature of the other. This might be schematically represented as follows:

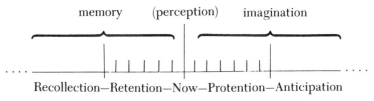

memory   (perception)   imagination

Recollection—Retention—Now—Protention—Anticipation

It is evident that, in terms of this emended model, imagining and remembering are co-constitutive of time-consciousness. This is all the more the case if it is true, as Derrida has recently argued, that there is no such thing as the unalloyed *perception* of the present; if so, our fundamental consciousness of time is wholly the work of imagination and memory.[13]

Yet the symmetry of the model is misleading. The following asymmetrical aspects of the experience of time must be acknowledged:

1. Imagination is often involved in our awareness of the past. As screen memories and *déjà vu* experiences most clearly illustrate, the past is as much constructed as it is reconstructed, and imagination is the source of the constructive element that appears in the form of hypotheses, fantasies, and variations on what actually happened. (Such, incidentally, was the significance of Freud's abandonment of the seduction theory of hysteria in 1897: gen-

uine memories could not be distinguished from imaginings masquerading as memories.)

2. While remembering always concerns itself with the past (or with what purports to belong to the past), imagining knows no comparable constriction in regard to the future. We can actively imagine the past (i.e., what the past was like) or the present (i.e., what is taking place *somewhere else* in the present). Indeed, we can imagine things that have no relationship at all with the past, present, or future regarded as three distinct phases of 'lower time'. *When* is the golden mountain I construct in imagination? At no designatable time: purely fictitious imagined objects are atemporal. And when imagining is extended in creative visualizing, what is experienced may present itself neither as temporal nor as atemporal, but as belonging to time of another order, e.g., to what Tarthang Tulku calls "Great Time."[14]

3. Just as imagining exceeds the confines of the anticipatable future, so remembering overruns the boundaries of the delimited past as described by Husserl. Memory extends not only to the immediate past (still 'reverberating' in retentional consciousness) and to the past recaptured in recollection (that is, the consolidated personal past which I revive in recall), but to another form of the past as well—the *immemorial* past that stretches beyond anything I have previously experienced in my personal past.[15] *Im-memorial* signifies what is not to be remembered in any usual way, that is, by retentive or recollective modes of rememoration. It is a matter of *anamnesis* or "reminiscence" in Plato's sense of the word: calling back to mind what was never before encountered as such in conscious experience. Here it is more than a question of acknowledging that imagination has more to do with Hades, and memory with Zeus, than is indicated by Husserl's antiseptic, Saturnine model. The whole model, and thus imagining and remembering as well, are subtended by an immemorial Chaos preceding ordered time.

IV

Time binds. Time, as it is consciously comprehended and experienced, keeps us confined to the personal past and future. These latter are knit together into a tight unity—a unity as tight as that of our defensively structured ego itself. Even as "life history," time is a binding force, and it is understandable that human temporality is so often viewed as a form of fallenness (and even as fallenness itself: Heidegger links *Verfallenheit* and *Zeitlichkeit*).[16] Likewise, the kind of history that recounts the collective experience of the past, seeing in it a mere sequence of events, is situated on still another horizontal timeline traversing lower or ordinary time.

But beyond the personal and collective past is a past which is expansive rather than contractive. Such a past is a timeless time, inchoate and antedating history or personal experience. It is a special case of Great Time, mythic in status, and its temporality is that of *in illo tempore:* in *that* time, a time before measurable, Chronic time. Such a time never was actual and is hence not remembered *as* actual. This means that it is not remembered at all in the usual sense. Rather, the mythic past is re-collected in an act of reminiscence whose content is impersonal or prepersonal: non-egological.[17] Re-*collected* from what?

Not from perception, thought, or personal memory, but from the *imagining* of archetypal presences. An archetypally enlivened imagination creates *imagines agentes* that move the soul. These active images are not projections of the future, nor even moving images of eternity. They are beyond *mimesis* just as they are beyond quantified time. Even if experienced *in* time, archetypally active images are themselves transtemporal, outside the self-enclosing limits of ordinary time. As such they remain objects of imagination, which is uniquely capable of leading us beyond determinate temporality.

Yet, when imagining becomes archetypal in its activity, it also has to do with presences that revive in consciousness by means of *anamnesis*. Although originally presented and structured in acts of imagining, these presences are re-experienced as re-collected *memoria*—as if they had already occurred or been experienced before. Which they have: *in imagination.* All significant human experiences are re-experiences.[18] This is the core of truth in Plato's theory that the objects of reminiscence have been encountered before, not in this life but in a form of preexistence which the soul alone has experienced. Soul, being immortal, *has been* in contact with what is immemorial, with what is truly archaic. But this archaic residuum is archetypal before it is eidetic: having first arisen before the fall into personal or historical time, it is chaotic and achronic before being made manifest in cosmic-idetic patterns of the sort which Plato and post-Platonists seek.

We are left, then, with a strange supermyth or myth of myths. The soul is driven to construct the myth of preexistence or preexperience in order to account for its sense of familiarity with archetypal presences that appear in and through the active images sustaining myths proper, the tales of the gods that are recounted and written down. But the archpresences themselves are the specific concern of an archetypal imagination which envisions entities and events preexisting finite, sublunar time. There is a profound circularity of the divine, of the gods. Our own delimited imagining, taking place in the present, rekindles divine presences which are felt to have been *toujours déjà là* and re-memberable as such. And they *have* always already been there, since an archetypally alive imagination has *never not been active* in putting them there. *This* imagination, which is the indefatigable demiurge of soul and which belongs to no one person (and perhaps to no *person* at all), undergirds our everyday imagining as surely as our more paltry powers of memory are underpinned by the anamnesic rememoration of which we are on occasion capable.[19]

The circularity in question is also, and ultimately, a circularity of imagination and memory themselves. The continuity of the archaic and the archetype, of pretemporality and atemporality, and of lower time and Great Time, represents a species of collaboration between imagining and remembering which Western philosophy has been loathe to recognize. Small wonder. For such an extraordinary collaboration of the two powers departs radically from the schema of horizontal and vertical axes discussed at the beginning of this essay. A truly re-collective memory and an archetypally active imagination conjoin forces in a manner that cannot be charted or contained by diachronic-synchronic perpendicularity. They combine in the conjoint work of soul-making, an opus that cannot be captured adequately by contrasting images of height and fallenness. In soul-making, time is not the time of the person or even of the world, but a time outside both, an acosmic time not representable by any axis or time line. It is a time out of mind, a time of soul, a Great Time made accessible by the complementary activities of imagining and remembering in their most profoundly circular co-agency. Yet it is a time not known or knowable as such: Great Time is the self. But the self cannot fathom Time.[20]

Notes

1. For we must distinguish the everlasting, i.e., indefinitely protracted duration, from the eternal, which is a sheerly static *nunc stans*. This distinction is already made by Plato at *Timaeus* 37–38.

2. On focal setting and partitioning, see Tarthang Tulku, *Time, Space, and Knowledge* (Emeryville, Calif.: Dharma Publishing, 1977), p. 85 and p. 125.

3. This is so even if the projection of the vertical axis onto the horizontal axis constitutes the essence of poetic language, as in Jakobson's conception. Cf. Roman Jakobson, "Linguistics and Poetics," in *The Structuralists*, ed. R. and F. De George (New York: Anchor, 1972), pp. 95–97. On the "endless diffusion" of 'lower time' on the lateral axis, see Tarthang Tulku, *Time, Space, and Knowledge*, pp. 137–39 and p. 171. On the horizontal character of lower time (i.e., "ordinary time"), see ibid., p. 145 and pp. 168–69.

4. An equally valid basis for contrast is suggested in Charles E. Scott's seminal discussion of archetypal differences between Zeus and Hades, aether and darkness, in his essay "Utter Darkness and Aether: The Elements of Hades and Zeus."

5. "Duration is but as it were the length of one straight line, extended *in infinitum*" (John Locke, *An Essay Concerning Human Understanding*, ed. Peter H. Nidditch [Oxford: at the Clarendon Press, 1975], p. 203). For Tarthang Tulku's discussion and critique of linear temporality, see *Time, Space, and Knowledge*, pp. 121–27, 136–41, and 181.

6. Heidegger finds Nietzsche's conception of *Rausch*, "ecstatic intoxication," to be central to the latter's conception of art and of Dionysus; see "Der Rausch als ästhetischer Zustand," in Martin Heidegger, *Nietzsche*, 2 vols. (Pfullingen: Neske, 1961), 1: 122 ff. In the light of what has just been said above, compare Heidegger's notion of the "round dance" (*Ringen*) of the fourfold figures (*das Geviert*)—wherein man and earth seem to arrange themselves on a horizontal axis and sky and gods on a vertical one. Cf. M. Heidegger, "Das Ding," in *Vorträge und Aufsätze* (Pfullingen: Neske, 1954).

7. Hobbes, *Leviathan*, ed. C. B. MacPherson (New York: Penguin, 1968), p. 89. Hobbes underlines *imagination* and *memory*.

8. Ibid.

9. On the originary, nonsecondary character of imagination and memory, see Tarthang Tulku, *Time, Space, and Knowledge*, passim. Cf. also my "Imagining and Remembering," *Review of Metaphysics* 31 (December, 1977), pp. 187–209, esp. sections I-III.

10. Cf. my *Imagining: A Phenomenological Study* (Bloomington: Indiana University Press, 1976), esp. chapters 8 and 9.

11. Edmund Husserl, *The Phenomenology of Internal Time-*

Consciousness, trans. James Churchill (Bloomington: Indiana University Press, 1964).

12. Ibid., p. 75. (*"Die Einheit des Erinnerten"* is the German phrase.)

13. Jacques Derrida, *Speech and Phenomena*, trans. David Allison (Evanston: Northwestern University Press, 1973), passim.

14. See Tarthang Tulku, *Time, Space, and Knowledge*, chapters 7, 8, 9, and esp. p. 156: "If we see 'things' as 'space' and 'time', *we can move and open through these dimensions to expose infinite fields of possibilities* within what seemed a finite encounter" (Tarthang Tulku's italics). It is evident that such fields of possibility are made available through active imagining, which has the purely possible as its proper object. (On this last point, see *Imagining*, chapter 5: "Indeterminacy and Pure Possibility.")

15. For exercises in which remembering is allowed to assume this transpersonal role, see Tarthang Tulku, *Time, Space, and Knowledge*, pp. 174–81 (esp. Exercises 18, 19, and 20).

16. " 'Spirit' does not fall *into* time; but factical existence 'falls' as falling *from* [*verfallende aus*] primordial, authentic temporality" (Martin Heidegger, *Being and Time*, trans. J. Macquarrie and E. Robinson [New York: Harper & Row, 1962], p. 486; Heidegger's italics). Cf. Tarthang Tulku's strikingly similar notion of the self as already fallen into lower time: *Time, Space, and Knowledge*, p. 166.

17. " 'Lower time' amounts to an attempted taming and appropriation of Great Time for egoistic purposes" (Tarthang Tulku, *Time, Space, and Knowledge*, p. 137).

18. "The finding of an object is in fact a refinding of it" (Sigmund Freud, *Standard Edition of the Complete Psychological Works*, ed. James Strachey, 24 vols. [London: Hogarth Press, 1953–74], 7:222). Compare with this strangely Platonic statement Tarthang Tulku's view that the self is "a patterning or embodying tendency of 'time', and *as such*, bears 'knowingness' throughout the full extent of its formation" (*Time, Space, and Knowledge*, p. 166; Tarthang Tulku's italics).

19. For further thoughts on such an imagination, see my two articles, "Toward an Archetypal Imagination," *Spring* (1974) and "Time in the Soul," *Spring* (1979).

20. Tarthang Tulku, *Time, Space, and Knowledge*, p. 170.

CHAPTER 5

It has been said that those who fail to learn the lessons of history are doomed to repeat them. In the article that follows, James Shultz suggests that while the social sciences have in fact uncovered one of history's most important teachings—namely, that the motivating and structuring forces in all social arrangements are beliefs, customs, and mores—we have not yet taken this lesson to heart. Nor, in his opinion, have we fully comprehended its importance in terms of the quality of our individual and collective existence.

Dr. Shultz points out that the patterns of history closely parallel those of human thought, and suggests that the conflict and repetition that have always been part of the social world reflect our reliance on a kind of knowledge that aims at establishing and defending fixed positions, a knowledge that is duplicative at its very core. It is not surprising then that the breakthroughs in the social sciences have been insufficient to teach us what we need to know. For, if the main social problem is the human tendency to proceed in terms of beliefs, the multiplying of conceptualizations cannot provide a remedy. What is needed, according to Dr. Shultz, is a far more comprehensive and incisive understanding of the workings of ordinary knowing.

Toward this end, he offers three exercises inspired by his study of *Time, Space, and Knowledge*. These allow one to see the extent to which the world has been run on beliefs and then to discover, 'within' the standard patterns themselves, a kind of 'knowing' that is both flexible and wholly in tune with the times. Even though this natural intelligence is not the sort of thing that can *belong* to any individual, or to any group of individuals, Dr. Shultz considers it as mankind's greatest resource. With it as a guide, the human race can, he thinks, transform its dreams into living realities.

As collateral reading, we recommend Part Three of *Time, Space, and Knowledge* and the Foreword to this anthology.

James Shultz

TIME, SPACE, AND KNOWLEDGE, Social Science, and the American Dream

Just as the atom, when investigated by natural scientists, was found to have spaces within it, so society and culture, when investigated by social scientists, was found to have enormous open spaces which often go unnoticed. Social science has investigated the seemingly solid surfaces of the social world and discovered that the opaque partitioning of human social environments and groups can be 'seen through'. The seemingly stable boundaries have turned out to be no more than mores, customs, beliefs, consumer preferences, habits, dress patterns, languages, and concepts of time and space. This insight about social 'space' finds a broader context in *Time, Space, and Knowledge*:[1]

> Everything in our lives and our history is received by the mind and senses. We usually are so outward-oriented and preoccupied with 'things' that we do not pay much attention to the fact (according to our ordinary view) that all 'things' are just what the mind shows us, what can be picked up by mind. Nor do we notice that everything can be analyzed and found to be given by a few common elements—sensings, images, words, concepts, interpretations,

verbal associations, memories . . . that is all there is to
our world! Duplication, rearrangements, modifications of
images and ideas—all 'mindings', nothing else! . . .
. . . Consider our educational process, social customs,
and entertainments. Look at the achievements and benefits of our overall trend. What have we actually accomplished? It seems to amount to only images, sensations, and
concepts . . . more 'mindings'. (p. 226)°

If it is difficult to notice that 'things' are picked up by
a certain type of knowing, it is equally difficult to notice
that the apparently substantial and real social world rests
upon 'mindings' and beliefs. Social science—anthropology,
sociology, history, economics, and political science—has
pointed out that the emperor has no clothes, that all social
phenomena are conditioned and relative; but it has often
countered old beliefs, 'by-standers', and 'outside-standers'
with new ones. (See p. 72.) Yet, as Herbert Guenther says
in the foreword to *Time, Space, and Knowledge,* "There is
not the slightest difference whether one is fettered by a
chain of gold or a rope of straw" (p. xx). From the standpoint of the Time-Space-Knowledge vision, there is no
pure or ultimate 'by-stander' or 'outside-stander' at the
social or cultural level. At one level of knowledge, certain
dogmas, opinions, beliefs, and customs may seem to be
better than some others, but each is a 'read-out' of a
particular focal setting.

The chain of gold offered by social science is the net-
work of its own answers, theories, concepts, laws, and

labels. Its practitioners have opened up commonsense assumptions by offering various abstractions, usually in reductionistic or objectivistic forms. And while they have shown that family ties depend upon various political and economic conditions (and vice versa), and that religious dogmas and political movements are all time- and culture-bound, social scientists have rarely examined the arbitrary and conventional partitions within their own disciplines from a holistic perspective.

Modern man may have less trouble (at least in principle) recognizing the insubstantial, spacelike character of all social phenomena, but most people still recoil, as if from a poisonous snake, when confronted with the radical freedom and openness implied by Great Space and Great Time. And this recoil is not limited to scientists and academicians. As new waves of immigrants, new contacts with an ever-wider world, and new discoveries have pointed out the arbitrariness of all our conventions and beliefs, we have responded by clinging all the more tightly to other partitions, identifications, labels, and positions— to machines, numbers, social roles, laws, addresses, and a seemingly endless profusion of new objects and possessions. All of this, however, seems to have taken us further away from appreciating our own nature and our physical environment. We are like the man eating froth who, when told it had no food value, tripled his intake.

Someday the social scientist, like the physicist, may end up focusing on time, space, and knowledge as central processes. Investigating societies and social systems, he may find that these are essentially time and space, and that being a social scientist is like trying to write with a finger in a swiftly moving river. He may also discover that working with anything less fluid and open than time and space leads to a 'science' trapped in partial locations—dogmas that are soon localized in narrow space, and soon behind the times. A thorough investigation may reveal only flashes of meaning—'laws', hypotheses, theories—surrounded by ever-widening space and time. (Such an investigation could be most useful, too, for loosening the usual social conventions, boundaries, and beliefs.)

This is what 'higher knowledge' might discover by writing in the river. Generally, however, the scientist rejects the fluidity and openness of the river and tries to find a more stable medium or a more 'precise' methodology. He either puts some of the river in a bottle and freezes it, or he avoids rivers altogether by defining truth to be whatever our concepts can capture or our tests can measure. But neither of these strategies can succeed, ultimately, since we and our social artifacts *are* the river, the vastness and openness of time, space, and knowledge. This perfectly pure river, beyond concepts, beliefs, and positions, includes both scientist and science, at the same time as it eludes them.

There are, however, practical ways to open up the social investigation. Two exercises, similar to those found in *Time, Space, and Knowledge*, follow as illustrations. Both draw on the social sciences and our current 'lower' knowledge. The reader may want to use the illustrative material as a takeoff point for exploring whatever comes to mind.

Exercise 1: Historical Overview

Visualize the long flow of human affairs based upon your knowledge of history, archeology, anthropology, economics, political science, and sociology. Try to see the biggest possible picture; but also try to empathize with the feelings and lived-worlds of people from all times and places.[2] Consider, for example, the following:

1. evolution
2. living in caves
3. living as nomads, hunters, gatherers
4. moving the extended family to find more space
5. families expanding geometrically, subdividing, growing into clans and tribes
6. conflicts between branches
7. kinship-based ties giving way, with increased settlement and population, to more diverse communities based on rituals, division of labor, and laws
8. the development of various oral and written languages
9. the proliferation of tools, including weapons
10. the rise of ever larger empires, such as those of Babylonia, Egypt, China, India, Persia, Macedonia (Alexander), Rome, England, USSR, USA
11. the gradually extending map of the known world
12. society differentiating into separated spheres of government, science, religion, and the arts
13. the rise of the modern industrial nations
14. the role of the mastery of military inventions and transportation in the rise of the West
15. ever more diversified technology
16. people from various lands coming to America seeking freedom and prosperity

17. various wars, famines, and epidemics
18. changing social customs, languages, codes of right and wrong
19. the shock to our liberal optimism about progress from World Wars I and II, the Nazi regime, totalitarian states, and nuclear bombs
20. the increasing 'mastery' of the environment paralleled by pollution, our using it up and our running it down
21. the way psychology treats human experience more and more as an object viewed from the outside

In contemplating this picture, draw on whatever ordinary knowledge comes to mind. Try to penetrate this knowledge and realize deeper level insights: the transience of all rulers, empires, and beliefs, the increasingly restricted sense of inner time and space, the crowding of outer time and space arising from a restricted focal setting, and so on.

Notice that restricted focal settings did not end with the Renaissance or with the decline of religion. Note the new dogmatisms—in obvious forms, such as communism and capitalism, and in subtle forms, like history's being taught during the twentieth century with little reference to the great, ancient cultures of India and China. Note how each culture's view of history was tied to its time and location, and how each culture reinforced and protected its conventional beliefs about the world. Note how "impervious" structures of belief and convention were later dissolved and how new structures arose, in turn, to be dissolved.

This fresh use of social science's 'lower' knowledge contrasts with the way such knowledge is usually presented, when the purpose is to establish premises or prove points, in the process of building up a maze of new beliefs and judgments. In the "Historical Overview," the same knowledge is used to investigate the openness of time and space and the limitations of *all* 'lower' knowledge—of all beliefs, concepts, conventions, and pretensions.

Exercise 2: Loosening Our Cultural Beliefs

Now extend the same process to the present worldwide, and especially American, society and culture. The same processes of 'minding' which were operative in the past are operative in the present. (At least this seems quite likely, unless we believe that we have somehow outgrown all the past tendencies to reify our ideas into inveterate structures, and to place our faith in beliefs, conventions, and dogmas.) Investigate some of the beliefs operative in our society—beliefs which seem to be the best that time and space have to offer, but which are actually produced by narrow focal settings.

Consider, for example, the assumptions common in the social sciences about linear time and the inadmissibility of all but certain kinds of evidence; they are, after all, beliefs and conventions. The confidence we have in our laws, economic systems, education, sciences, and technologies are also beliefs, as are the adversarial attitudes we tend to take toward the environment and toward one another. Consider that reacting emotionally and sensationally, with a short time perspective, is fostered by our mass media and that it hampers our ability to play a stable, dependable role in the larger international scene.

One of the deepest assumptions is that our 'good' or 'better' economic and political systems will protect us from the difficulties that usually befall empires and cultures. Consider the belief that our institutions will somehow rise above or compensate, in the long run, for human frailties like selfishness; that laws will be better than the people; that egocentric, shortsighted pursuit of self-interest will ultimately produce a cooperative society; that shouting and pushing for one's unexamined opinions will work out to be best for everyone. Such assumptions are often defended by saying that our systems are as good as anyone else's. Though true at one level, this amounts to the belief that, however incomplete, the present version of social life is the best that time, space, and knowledge can offer.

While it is important not to reify the more limiting aspects of our culture and society, it may be useful to sensitively investigate its limitations, without glossing over matters or adopting a skeptical or cynical position. For example, one might consider the following:

1. the increasing demarcation of land, work, and social structures into defined territories
2. the role of mass propaganda in controlling beliefs and preferences
3. America's past and present role in the world, and the world's response to America
4. prevalent attitudes toward the physical, psychological, and social environment

5. the gap between the preferred picture of life and the way people experience it

6. the sources and costs of the GNP

7. the way that most jobs and entertainments act against awareness and wider perspectives by keeping one busy, occupied, and enclosed in a small space

8. the role of solidified beliefs in wars, class conflicts, other strife

9. the element of self-centeredness in our idea of freedom and our choice of economic and political policies

10. the various definitions of success and their ramifications

11. the groups left out, such as older people

12. the failure of the modern industrial world to satisfy desires for larger space and the time to enjoy it

13. the attitude of the modern world toward the heritage of human values

14. the various confusions and contradictions about freedom and democracy

15. the ambivalent relation of Americans to 'authority'

In completing exercise 2, the specific questions you ask, the examples you consider, and the explorations you conduct can be opened up, since these too are 'mindings' and beliefs. Also, the slant in exercise 2 toward limitations might be countered by simultaneously focusing on potentials—signs of openness to greater knowledge, space, and time within American culture and society. The purpose of exploring limitations is to loosen up beliefs, not to create a new system of negative, cynical, and skeptical beliefs.

These exercises may serve to open up the investigation of social phenomena further than usual. In addition to the general insight that all social phenomena are insubstantial expressions of time, space, and knowledge, a specific understanding emerges of the role of beliefs in all human affairs, and of the arising of all beliefs within an insufficient appreciation of time, space, and knowingness.

The world of human affairs has been run largely on beliefs. Most fundamental among our beliefs is the view that we are lacking something in our lives and must 'get' fulfillment. Time and again this 'getting' has been tied up with a thousand other beliefs and modes of behavior to which we must conform. These beliefs, prejudices, partial confrontations, and 'objective facts' avoid the main existential issues of being in the world. In being run this way, the world has been run poorly; it has been run down.

How much dignity, inner harmony, or integration with nature has been achieved? How many people can see life as a great gift—as the performance of a profoundly celebratory drama?

History continually witnesses both dissatisfaction with the world and attempted transcendences of it. Many attempts to transcend it, as well as to 'improve' the world and the lot of mankind, have been institutionalized on a large scale. But these attempts have all been based on *beliefs*, rather than on an investigation concerning the nature of true value, virtue, and balance.

Beliefs . . . uncertainly . . . doubts . . . protective entrenchment against doubt . . . factions . . . enforcement and bribes to stay in line . . . threats . . . guilt . . . fear . . . resultant dishonesty with others *and* oneself . . . divisiveness . . . subtle schizophrenia . . . franticness . . . hope and fear together—

tremendous pressure
pervading everything—
habituation
so we don't even notice it.

In such circumstances
who can directly and sensitively
face
what life offers? . . .

This oppressive history is an indication of the magnitude of our present dilemma. We are in a position to take stock of this whole trend. At some deep psychological level we have already done this, and are tired now, tired to an ultimate degree. We are bored with the whole show. Our fundamental difficulties are *not* being resolved, and we can see this clearly. . . .

So far we have been perfect believers. What is the remedy? 'Knowledge', inner intelligence, vigorous appreciation! With these available, it becomes possible to use the elements of our realm in a positive way. (pp. 227–30)

In extending this investigation of beliefs further, we might look at some of those that are most basic to our society—beliefs which, when they are not being lived, lead to a pervasive sense of 'lostness', or confusion, or wasting time. Perhaps these fundamental ideas, when taken together, could be called the *American Dream*. Even those who have rejected this dream may still be controlled by it in rebelling against it or in trying to escape from it by searching for some new, non-American religious or political system. Perhaps a more thorough investigation is warranted—of what the cultural aspiration has been, how it is faring now, where it is headed, and how to go beyond it.

One aspect of the American Dream has been the vision that society has the potential to unite all kinds of people in cooperation and community, and to break through the walls of race, clan, language, creed, class, and so on.

O beautiful for spacious skies,
For amber waves of grain,
For purple mountain majesties
Above the fruited plain.
America! America! God shed His grace on thee,
And crown thy good with brotherhood
From sea to shining sea.

Another aspect of the vision is the belief that liberty and freedom can be actualized for the greater happiness and well-being of all.

My country, 'tis of thee,
Sweet land of liberty,
Of thee I sing;
Land where my fathers died,
Land of the Pilgrims' pride,
From ev-'ry mountain side,
Let freedom ring.

Underlying this dream of community and freedom is the sense of a beautiful, spacious land. This land, and the people's hard labor, are the bases for a third aspect of the dream—a vision of the earth bringing forth prosperity for all, at whatever level their effort deserves, and of the resulting material progress leading to greater human happiness.

These three attributes of the American Dream seem to share an openness, pointing to higher knowledge and larger time and space. In a sense, the definitions of freedom and democracy, and the notion of a community that transcends ethnocentrism, arose from the founders' knowing recognition of the limits of all opinions, ideologies, and rulers. So, too, the idea of prosperity based on self-reliance and creativity arose.

Thus the American Dream was essentially an opening process, but the elements were soon reified and progressively reduced to standard conventions and beliefs. In itself, the vision of freedom points to inner freedom, that of community points to compassion and equality (all being equally part of time, space, and knowledge), and the vision of prosperity points to greater human joy and happiness—to everything that fully satisfies and fulfills the human mind.

But the openness of these visions consolidated and froze into a labyrinth of formalities and impervious surfaces, typical of lower knowledge. Unknowingness showed itself in separation, divisiveness, heedlessness toward the environment, diversions, personal power, possessions, and the other trends as explored in exercise 2, above. The inner freedom that underlies the conventional freedom of movement and thought was allowed to deteriorate; the wider perspective and sense of community underlying a truly open, democratic society were neglected and replaced by a standardized mass market; the deeper sources of satisfaction and fulfillment were sacrificed to a frantic search for possessions or locations. Now, however, we are running short of resources—partly because the rest of the world has been following the American example.

Though the original vision of America was relatively open, there were also biases which led to painful encounters with lower time and space. The concept of freedom, for example, was emptied of content; it became 'freedom from', but not 'freedom for'. (If one asks about content, the response is generally made that no one should force his values on another—a valid point but hardly the end of the investigation.) This kind of freedom has often meant a decline in civility and community, and an increase in isolation and selfishness; people who are only interested in being free *from* quickly lose any sensitivity beyond the 'personal' sphere. Even though this form of liberty supports freedom of movement and thought, its limits become apparent within the organizations and social structures where people spend much of their lives. We see, for instance, the constant social manipulation of people as consumers of things, ideas, services, and entertainments, so that "doing one's own thing" may just reflect fitting in.

The emphasis on solving material problems through science and technology has had useful results, but shortcomings of this approach are becoming more apparent, especially as other societies, chasing the American Dream, abandon their ancient heritages and, with them, their ties to the deeper values of humanity. Perhaps, unwittingly, we have done the same. There certainly is a widespread feeling that there is little room left for, and that time is running out on, the American Dream; and this has produced confusion, conflict and general disappointment within American society. Perhaps the Time-Space-Knowledge vision can help us find access to accommodating perspectives, allowing space for us to breathe, by transcending the usual dichotomies between spiritual and material, capitalist and communist, modern and traditional, democratic and autocratic.

Exercise 3: Beyond Culture and History

Envision the openness of space expressed in the sky, the sun's rays, the earth, the mountains, and the ocean.

Extend this openness until it contacts the space 'within' you. Feel the relaxed, neutral, joyful, and complete experience of your own nature blending with the purity of the sky, the ocean, the mountans of 'outer' nature. Visualize this as the essence of the human experience, untouched by nation, era, or religion. Extend this same openness to societies and social relationships. Envision these as being Great Space and Time, balanced, harmonious, in tune with human fulfillment and with nature.

Exercise 3 points beyond any esoteric discipline, any new or old spiritual system or dogma; these too are enveloped in beliefs and conventions. It is like the unbiased, open mind of true science, like the "inner kingdom" of the Judeo-Christian vision, like the deep experiencing that is the goal of those seeking philosophical or psychological insight. It contacts higher knowledge which reflects Great Space and Time. Like the Hebrew *Yahweh*, this higher knowledge 'judges' and loosens the pretensions of all social systems and restores the vision needed to see opportunities and potentialities for human fulfillment in the future.

Time, Space, and Knowledge offers materials that help free the mind from its more or less narrow approach to social and cultural phenomena. It asks us to experiment with opening to a dimension which is not a viewpoint maintained by 'outside-standers' or 'by-standers'. If we can contact sensitive, appreciative intimacy—if we can learn to use time, space, and knowledge wisely—then perhaps we can accomplish more than any human beings have throughout history.

The main social problem seems to be that of becoming stuck in our beliefs. We do not go beyond beliefs; we do not stay open long enough, deep enough. Once we believe something, we are stuck, and then we experience isolation, disharmony, and freezing. More conflict occurs, we fail to respect each other's cultures, and our own becomes more rigid. But in this new, cross-cultural time, we have the opportunity to open up and learn. The quality of society depends directly on the prevalent 'minding'. To be an open, balanced society, we must deal with bureaucratization of the mind itself, not just with externals. Openness goes beyond emotions and concepts of time and space. Religions, sciences, and governments differ, but the essential process of dogma is the same: it cannot accommodate. As an invitation to accommodation, the *Time, Space, and Knowledge* approach is not another new doctrine; it is neither anti nor pro, but just helps to lubricate. There is nothing wider or more permitting than space, time, and knowingness.

Time, Space, and Knowledge points beyond any kind of ethnocentric positions or social lines to a new potential for education—learning for cooperation, understanding, inner freedom, and the ability to live happily without wasting resources. The *Time, Space, and Knowledge* vision emphasizes the failure to clearly perceive our relation to time (so that our views are always behind the times) and the failure to perceive space (so that we set up tight boundaries and fixed positions which we then have to defend). Setbacks to the American Dream are signals that the opening process did not go far enough; it did not open up the fundamental beliefs underlying our culture. *Time, Space, and Knowledge* can help challenge these beliefs, loosening standard assumptions constructively and practically, not skeptically and not abstractly.

If higher knowledge is possible, even natural, then how did we lose it? Perhaps our treatment of nature, manipulative and adversarial, was reflected inside, as the way we treated ourselves, and outside, as the way we treated each other. We separated intellect from aesthetic perception and sensation from intuition. The more natural knowingness was also the highest, but we did not realize this, and so we created ("discovered") more and more formulations and reductions. (There were more books published in the last forty years than in the rest of man's history.)

This 'knowledge' led to some new openings, but overall, it narrowed our perceptions of space, time, and ourselves. We cannot renew our contact with 'higher knowledge' through more reductions, extremes, and opinions. We cannot 'grasp' higher knowledge, and yet it is very near and may be the essence of the American Dream and the real spirit of democracy—a lucid, balanced opening. It is not just ideals and systems, but people listening and sharing in an unselfish, open-minded, and patient way. Without this spirit, democracy, if it remains noncoercive, becomes chaotic and loses its direction. Intelligence must go beyond just defending one's own position and arguing for one's own ideas. Intelligence must rely on appreciative perception, not just on beliefs and doctrines. In this way, it can have a unifying, communicating quality based on sensitive feeling and empathy.

This process of opening up, of nonbelief and nonconcept, is not a sheer nothing; it is an important *doing*. When 'I' is 'you', as part of the same time, space, and knowledge, we can share and work together more freely. Prosperity can have a rich yet natural sweetness, like nectar. If the nectar reaches us and we taste it, we will know that it is not an abstraction or an impossibility. Then we may not be so bothered by small things. Society will work more effectively when our minds become more lucid.

The importance of knowledge points to the role of education. Education can be more than language, numbers, secondhand opinions and beliefs. It can create the lucid, sensitive, and feeling mind needed for seeing larger pictures. This higher knowledge can communicate, harmonize, and lead in new directions—toward a healthy, meaningful existence, and a wholeness beyond self and world. It sees the whole earth and all beings, and it sees through the various artificial partitions caused by beliefs that were merely premature closures of our intelligence. Time, space, and knowledge allow everything to unfold, and so allow more depth and fulfillment—just as they allow any amount of consolidating and freezing.

Since society itself reflects 'mindings', if there are deeper insights, there can be a different society. This is why the *Time, Space, and Knowledge* vision, while pointing out the limitations of conventional knowledge, is not pessimistic. We *can* improve on what we've been given; progress is possible. The main restrictions are our focal settings—deeper than lifestyle, geography, politics, class, race, country, but capable of being limited by any of these. We can look beyond these focal settings, however, and see that what is familiar is continuous with a more fundamental space and time.

For we already have the freedom to explore other levels of knowledge, a freedom we can experience directly, not just abstractly through some new 'outside-stander' or 'by-stander'. If used wisely, it can lead us to an incisive understanding of the global level as the natural freedom of time, space, and knowingness—an understanding that can overcome the prevalent divisiveness. It can lead us to find natural balance and harmony within both the social world and nature. This unifying perspective is like the sky which, though it seems 'empty', is a source of life.

Western social scientific knowledge has opened new frontiers, but has also contributed to the narrowing of our space and time into a linear, segmented view of mind, self, and world. An overall improvement in the human situation has not resulted so far. This is not altogether surprising, of course, since opening up the seemingly hard reality of human affairs is not just an intellectual task. Nor does it imply 'structural' solutions, if these simply reify some new focal setting: the ingrained tendency to believe, consolidate, and reify is already the main human social problem.

The American Dream of freedom, community, and prosperity requires an opening to freer knowingness, and to larger space and time. This opening can promote a light, artistic source of wonderment that has the natural qualities of sharing, which supports community; of inner freedom, which helps us to use and protect the gift of outer, legal freedom; and of harmony and balance, which support prosperity through the enjoyment of time, space, and natural resources.

At its best, the American Dream was never just American. It was and is an opening process, available to all, that can continue until it emerges within the knowingness of Great Space and Time.

> When a single feather and a thousand worlds
> Are equally this Space,
> Who can say which contains which?
> Who can find limits
> To life's richness? (p. xli)

> It is possible to open in a new way. We can venture into unmappable regions without relying on the usual essential cognitive hardware and categories, because everything and everywhere 'is' *Knowledge*. 'Knowingness' can handle *all* knowledge, continually finding more of itself and ever-greater life and fullness. (p. 231)

Notes

1. Tarthang Tulku, *Time, Space, and Knowledge: A New Vision of Reality* (Emeryville, Calif.: Dharma Publishing, 1977).

2. Before practicing this exercise, you may find it useful to look through one or more of the following:

(i) an introductory textbook in World History or World Civilization,

(ii) encyclopedia articles on specific cultures and societies,

(iii) selections from *History of Mankind: Cultural and Scientific Development*, International Commission for a History of the Scientific and Cultural Development of Mankind, 6 vols. (London: G. Allen and Unwin, 1963–76), or,

(iv) a historical atlas, such as the *Historical Atlas of the World* (New York: Barnes and Noble, 1972).

CHAPTER 6

Few people, save professional academics, have heard of Maurice Merleau-Ponty, and even fewer have studied his writings. Yet, this French philosopher-psychiatrist was undoubtedly among the most brilliant and original thinkers of the twentieth century. The historical importance of Merleau-Ponty's work is undisputed, for it constituted a turning point in the development of phenomenology. But beyond that, his thought provides an understanding of human being that, in itself, has the power to awaken one to much that lies 'hidden' in experience.

Merleau-Ponty saw the task of phenomenology as that of revealing "the mystery of the world and of reason," and his explorations did, indeed, turn up much that seems rather mysterious at first sight. He speaks of a "global bodily knowledge which systematically embraces all of its parts," and of the body itself as "essentially an expressive space." Perception he found to be a sort of "communion" between an object, which is inseparable from the one perceiving it, and a subject, which is time. Merleau-Ponty's analysis of time, then, disclosed "subject and object as two abstract 'moments' of a unique structure which is presence."

Even though these statements may seem unusual from an ordinary perspective, they will be strikingly familiar to readers of *Time, Space, and Knowledge*. And in the commentary on Merleau-Ponty's *Phenomenology of Perception* that follows, David Levin explores these and many other parallels in considerable detail. (What appears here is part of a longer work that also investigates connections between Merleau-Ponty's phenomenology and Buddhist philosophy.)

But for all the likenesses he finds, Dr. Levin also sees fundamental differences. It is, for example, one thing to understand, as Merleau-Ponty did, that subject and object form an inseparable pair; it is quite another to *experience* and *embody* that understanding in a way that transforms our existence. However, with the assistance of the *Time, Space, and Knowledge* exercises, Dr. Levin believes that we can come to realize the truth of Merleau-Ponty's insights in our own lives.

For further discussions of *Time, Space, and Knowledge* and phenomenology, please see the papers by D. Beere, E. Casey, and R. Romanyshyn. Dr. Beere's paper, in particular, should prove useful to readers who are unfamiliar with the methods and principles of phenomenology.

David Michael Levin

Tarthang Tulku and Merleau-Ponty

An Intertextual Commentary

Introduction

Maurice Merleau-Ponty, one of France's greatest philosophers—perhaps her greatest, along with Descartes—died in May, 1961, very suddenly and at the very height of his powers. But his project continues. In this commentary, for example, the project faces in the direction of Tibet, the Land of the Snows, the homeland of Buddhist teachers like Tarthang Tulku, who bring us the philosophy and psychology of their ancient tradition.

Being a reflection of the character of human experience, philosophy and psychology inevitably repeat certain inveterate tendencies. Their history, as Heidegger demonstrates, is a history of the suppression of feeling and the loss of perceptive awareness. Is there any way for the critical spirit within these disciplines to reverse this direction? It is my conviction that, thanks to Merleau-Ponty, we can begin to unravel this historical sequence, recovering that great potential for openness and relationship which still claims us in our being.

Merleau-Ponty's thinking, significant traces of which are embodied in his book *Phenomenology of Perception*, has not yet received from its native culture the depth of appreciation it deserves.[1] Perhaps that fuller appreciation will first come from those among us here who are now sharing the precious wisdom that arose and flourished in the East. However that may be, this much seems certain: Merleau-Ponty's phenomenology of embodiment provides an understanding of human being that is essential, and will be decisive, for a future blossoming of philosophy and psychology—for a new age, in which the powerful wisdoms of the two great hemispheres, East and West, are gathered together in one harmonious surge of energy, restoring everywhere an order that feels good, clearing a space-time field for the beauty of truth in its sensuous presencing, and creating a world of peace, where spontaneous love and compassion assure all beings of happiness and intrinsic fulfillment.

I offer here an intextual commentary: a commentary on Merleau-Ponty's *Phenomenology of Perception*, for readers who are familiar with Tarthang Tulku's *Time, Space, and Knowledge*[2] and feel motivated to understand their own experience of that vision more deeply with the help of Merleau-Ponty. The best way to use this commentary is to read it in conjunction with the *Phenomenology of Perception*. To encourage, and also assist, that kind of reading, I have ordered my commentary so that it follows the customary movement of reading. (Thus, the boldfaced numbers which begin the commentary units refer the reader to pages in Merleau-Ponty's text.) Nevertheless, for the reader who does not wish to undertake such an arduous reading, the commentary by itself will hopefully have some value.

The reading of Merleau-Ponty that I am proposing is intended to open up the text, letting it be heard in a new way. Once heard in this way, it will begin to articulate, contact, and express important dimensions of experience that are not so familiar to us, especially if we have not been practicing meditation for a long time—dimensions that may have been, until then, unnoticed, inaccessible, or even, perhaps, suppressed. The new way of hearing will facilitate, I believe, a deeper experience, and a clearer understanding, of the entire Buddhist tradition: of the *Abhidharma*, which concerns our capacity for feeling and perceptivity; of the *Madhyamika*, which guides us through the processes of opening and closing, reification and change, polarization and integration, division and wholeness; of the *Mahayana*, which kindly bends us toward the practice of compassion; and of the *Vajrayana*, which teaches these things by working in the most direct, most efficient way with our experience-as-we-live-it. Most especially, though, I believe that working with the Merleau-Ponty text will make some aspects of *Time, Space, and Knowledge*—Tarthang Tulku's wonderfully fresh vision, creative both in theory and in practice—more accessible than they might otherwise be.

In his preface to *Phenomenology of Perception*, Merleau-Ponty asserts that the task of phenomenology is "to reveal the mystery of the world and of reason" (*PP*, p. xxi). A careful reading of this work, in conjunction with the philosopher's other writings, makes it clear, moreover, that the ultimate goal of phenomenology is, for him, the attainment of a deeper self-understanding, bringing with it the enhancement and enrichment of human life. As a method for deepening our self-knowledge and expanding our understanding of the world, phenomenology helps us to contact the sleeping potential that lies hidden in the depths of our experience, and it facilitates the process of growth whereby we realize the richness of these depths. Phenomenology, as Merleau-Ponty understands it, is a process of opening. In this sense, doing phenomenology, like going into meditation, contributes to the meaningfulness, the value, of all existence. For doing phenomenology, like meditation, is simply a way of working with one's experience.

Commentary

54: Merleau-Ponty writes:

> The notion of geometrical space, indifferent to its contents, that of pure movement which does not by itself affect the properties of the object, provided phenomena with a setting of inert existence in which each event could be related to physical conditions responsible for the changes occurring, and therefore contributed to this *freezing of being* which appeared to be the task of physics. (Italics added.)

We now realize that the space of Euclidean geometry is only one among many other equally coherent, equally possible spaces. Other geometries, with different axioms, generate different theories of space. We also are beginning to realize, thanks to Einstein's Theory of Relativity, that the space of Newtonian physics is in many ways a freezing or solidification of a space which, from a no less scientific point of view, is inherently dynamic, mutable, and by no means uniform and homogeneous.

The phenomenological revolution, returning us to our *experiencing* of space, is not only consonant with these new and liberating developments in geometry and physics, but actually helps to explain them and make them intelligible. For it shows how our *sciences* of space originate in spatial *experience* and progressively develop through the processes of abstraction, idealization, and systematic formalization. At the same time, however, phenomenology also discloses that narrowness and frozenness are characteristic of even our ordinary, everyday experience of space. It thereby shows how the reductions of space accomplished by Euclidean geometry and Newtonian physics are already implicit in, and already prepared for by, the everyday way of experiencing space—the way that Edmund Husserl described, without presuming to judge it, as "the natural attitude."

Merleau-Ponty's work will show us, then, that our experience of space in the natural attitude is already, in itself, a *reduction*. Plumbing the depths of our experience as we live it, his phenomenology aims at liberating us from the confinement and pressure of this attitude and from the negative space into which it locks us. (Cf. chap. 1 and pp. 32–34.)*

55: It is traditional for philosophers to distinguish the nature of mind (cognitive activity) from the nature of body

---

*This and all the parenthetical page references that follow are to *Time, Space, and Knowledge,* unless otherwise noted.—ED.

(sensory experience) by characterizing the former as active, spontaneous, and creative, while calling the latter passive, receptive, and incapable of giving birth to meaning or value. (Cf. pp. 84–85.) Merleau-Ponty begins to question this distinction. He shows that sensory experience is always already involved with structures of meaning; it is never simply passive and receptive. And he helps us to focus on the receptive nature of sensation and perception: "Sense experience, thus detached from the affective and motor functions, became the mere reception of a quality, and physiologists thought they could follow, from the point of reception to the nervous centres, the projection [i.e., the imprint] of the external world in the living body."

Time, Space, and Knowledge takes us beyond the point where Merleau-Ponty leaves us. (See chap. 7, esp., pp. 153 and 159–62. Also see pp. 30–34 and 102–8.) For it asks us to *focus* on this reception as an experience. How does it feel? What kind of reception, what kind of welcome, are we giving to that which presents, or gives itself, to our senses? How our senses receive, how they greet what is given to them makes a significant difference. If we greet what comes to our senses with an attitude of joy, openness, praise, and thanksgiving, it stands to reason that our 'guests', the 'presents' which Western philosophers are all too fond of calling 'sense data' or 'sensory stimuli', will be pleasing and will make us very rich with their gifts of sensuous meaning. But if our gates of perception are partially closed, and our attitude is aversive, hostile, and unwelcoming, our 'visitors' will be likely to *reciprocate* that greeting. (See pp. 165–74 and exercise 30, pp. 258–

59). Our everyday habits of receiving sensory experience actually ensure a loss of sensuous meaning and value. We are ourselves responsible for a much-impoverished sensory experience. Depending on the quality and character of our reception, we either welcome or deny ourselves what Mikel Dufrenne calls "an apotheosis of the sensuous."[3]

By focusing on our sensory reception, *Time, Space, and Knowledge* shows how we have needlessly *reduced* the openness of experiential awareness; and it suggests ways to expand that awareness, so that we can greet and receive a much richer, much more wonderful present.

67: Merleau-Ponty asserts "that it is necessary to put the surroundings in abeyance the better to see the object, and to lose in background what one gains in focal figure. . . ." This is indeed true of our everyday experience, and especially of vision. But is it *necessarily* true? Is it true to the very depths of our experience? True to our potential? *Time, Space, and Knowledge* suggests a way of transcending this karmic cycle of causes and effects, where a gain here means a loss there. (See p. 59 and pp. 91–96.) Can we go beyond such duality? Can we escape the mental set which locks us into experiential habits that inevitably differentiate and polarize experience, so that we are *bound* to be left very frustrated and unsatisfied? The *Time, Space, and Knowledge* meditations teach us an *alternative* way of focusing, and, correspondingly, an *alternative* way of experiencing the background, so that we can escape being *caught* in a negative pattern of loss and gain. (See pp. 66–67 and pp. 126–32.)

68: Pursuing the subject of perception further, Merleau-Ponty says:

> To see is to enter a universe of beings which *display themselves*, and they would not do this if they could not be hidden behind each other or behind me. In other words: to look at an object is to inhabit it, and from this habitation to grasp all things in terms of the aspect which they present to it. But in so far as I see those things, too, they remain abodes *open to my gaze*, and, *being potentially lodged in them*, I already perceive *from various angles* the central object of my present vision. *Thus every object is the mirror of all others.* (Italics added. Cf. pp. 281–90, and exercises 29 and 30, pp. 257–59.)

Strictly speaking, is this true of our everyday vision in the natural attitude? I think not. But Merleau-Ponty's phenomenology goes deeper; it is not limiting itself to being true only of our most superficial, most restricted way of experiencing. Here, clearly, he is saying something intended to be true to the very depths of our experience. It is true, I think, to our inborn *potential* for enlightened vision. Being true to this potential, his phenomenology has the power to touch and move us; it has the power to release that potential, so that we may begin to realize the full richness of our capacity for vision.

Time, Space, and Knowledge offers numerous meditation practices (e.g., visualizing ourselves at another place and then 'moving' back and forth—exercise 20, p. 175) to help us with this realization. If we could somehow reach a point where we actually *see* every object mirroring all the others, our experience of space would greatly expand. If we could really *feel* ourselves already 'lodged' in the various things which surround the object of our focus, then the dualistic polarizations of experience into subject-object, this-that, and here-there would be loosened and relaxed, and we might begin to feel the beautiful *openness* of space and behold, in the play of reflections, shadows, echoes, and mimicries, the wonderful *depth* of things— and the harmonies of Nature.

69: "What we have just said about the spatial perspective," he avers, "could equally be said about the temporal." When we consider the field character of time, and the way each moment is related to all others, we may realize that, in fact, we have *always* lived, and thus *already* live, in the whole of time. And yet, how fully do we experience time in this wonderful way?

> The present still holds on to the immediate past *without positing it as an object,* and since the immediate past similarly holds its immediate predecessor, *past time is wholly collected up and grasped in the present.* The same is true of the imminent future which will also have its horizon of imminence. But with my immediate past I have also the horizon of futurity which surrounded it, and thus *I have my actual present seen as the future of the past.* With the imminent future, I have the horizon of past which will surround it, and therefore *my actual present as the past of that future.* (Italics added.)

How can we learn to *enjoy* the past, still present in (and as) its absence, without holding on to it (i.e., without clinging to it) as an object? How can we develop our ability to *feel* the past as wholly collected up and preserved in the present? How can we deepen our experience of the fact that we already 'have' with us our entire future? How can we clarify and deepen our vision, so that we really *see* our actual present as the future of the past? How can we so extend our vision, our sense of time, that we become capable of enjoying the actual present very deeply, so deeply, in fact, that we can *see* it as the past of our future?

There are a number of practices in *Time, Space, and Knowledge* (exercises 17–22, pp. 172–84) which address these very questions in a way that gives us a *direct experiential confirmation*, a personal realization that what Merleau-Ponty says is indeed true—true to our potential for a better-feeling experience of time, more open, more dynamic and expansive, and thus less oppressive. (See chap. 6, pp. 117–32.)

98: The first ten exercises in *Time, Space, and Knowledge* (pp. 21–39) ask us to visualize, in greater and greater detail, the structures of a giant human body. Readers wanting a clearer conceptual understanding of the visualization process should pay special attention to Merleau-Ponty's discussion in the chapter called "The Spatiality of One's Own Body and Motility." This discussion of the "body image" moves us much closer to an understanding of the process in which the visualization of an ideal body could serve as a schema (Kantian "schematization") for a different embodiment of space. (See also Merleau-Ponty's essay, "The Child's Relations with Others," published in *The Primacy of Perception*,[4] This essay has a good deal to say about the corporeal schema, the specular image and mirror, and "postural impregnation.")

105: Discussing the case of Schneider, diagnosed as suffering from damage to the brain, Merleau-Ponty notes that the patient's gesture "loses the melodic character which it presents in ordinary life, and becomes manifestly a collection of partial movements strung laboriously together." Schneider's movements thus come to resemble, or to exemplify, the Cartesian and materialist theories about the nature of human movement. But Schneider is suffering an impaired condition. For the first time since Plato and Aristotle, Western philosophy has a way of characterizing human movement that does not atomize it into a series of discrete and intrinsically meaningless motions.

But *Time, Space, and Knowledge* suggests the possibility that even our everyday movements and gestures may involve a loss of melodic character, a certain loss of grace. Why is it that our walking does not have a lively, dancing quality? Helping us to discover within our body the potential for such joyful and meaningful movement, movement wholly integrated into and wholly attuned to its situation, *Time, Space, and Knowledge* shows us another way of being in space. (See pp. 207–8, pp. 285–87 and exercise 34, pp. 275–77.) "Each instant of the movement," says Merleau-Ponty, describing a potential we rarely realize, "embraces its whole span" (*PP*, p. 140). Does our movement normally feel like an "embrace"? Only now and then, I think—when we find our stride, for instance. The *Time, Space, and Knowledge* exercises (for example, practice in slow walking, exercise 23, pp. 185–86) make use of the relationship between motility ("motor intentionality") and the experience of space to motivate desirable changes, especially with regard to the *feeling* of space.

132: Still discussing movement, Merleau-Ponty describes how "physiognomic perception" motivates movement: "the normal subject penetrates into the object by perception, assimilating its structure into his substance, and through this body the object directly regulates his movements." Does Merleau-Ponty's description accurately characterize our experience? To a degree, perhaps. But, with a little well-focused reflection, I think we would want to say that the "subject-object dialogue," as Merleau-Ponty calls it, could really be much less dualistic, much less polarized than it 'normally' is for us. The practices which *Time, Space, and Knowledge* gives us (for example, the subject-object reversal, exercise 30, p. 258, and the object-glow visualization, exercise 17, p. 172) can help us to deepen our experience of penetration and assimilation, so that we realize the nondual integratedness that Merleau-Ponty has described.

146: "Now the body is essentially an expressive space." The body *is* space, is the *same* as space, is not *other* than space. But it is a special 'moment', 'style', 'manner', or 'modulation' of space: the human body is space which is wonderfully *expressive*. It is enfolded space *expressing itself*. Elsewhere, Merleau-Ponty writes: "The body is not primarily *in* space: it is of it" (*PP*, p. 148). (See chap. 2, pp. 21–46.)

149: Having conducted a 'private' experiment, that anyone can repeat for himself, Merleau-Ponty notes:

When I am sitting at my table, I can instantly visualize the parts of my body which are hidden from me. As I contract my foot in my shoe, I can see it. This power belongs to me even with respect to parts of the body which I have never seen. . . . Thus . . . we immediately recognize the visual representation of what is invisible to us in our own body. . . . Each of us sees himself as it were through an inner eye. . . . (Compare this with the "Giant Body" visualization practice, pp. 21–30.)

Merleau-Ponty makes these points in the context of a chapter concerned with "the synthesis of one's own body." This synthesis is necessary, because without it there *is* no experiential body. The visualization he refers to, though much more limited than that proposed in *Time, Space, and Knowledge*, is a capacity made possible by the fact that vision is not a separate, isolated sense, but emerges from a *primordial, felt, sensory awareness* of our own body. This awareness is in its essence synthetic, integrative.

We can visualize "invisible" bodily interiors precisely because we are talking about the 'phenomenal body', or the 'experiential body', the body I am, the body I live; and because the interdependencies and syntheses which constitute the essence of this body *involve* the immanent power to visualize in felt processes of meaningfulness, such as movements, gestures, expressions, postures. But *Time, Space, and Knowledge* proposes to take this capacity for "corporeal schematization" much further, by means of disciplined exercises and practice. Merleau-Ponty's phenomenological analysis helps clarify how (why) visualization is possible; his discussion of the "corporeal schema" in "The Child's Relations with Others" (in *The Primacy of Perception*), is also useful in elucidating the visualization process. But he does not appreciate how this very important phenomenological fact, introduced mainly in order to make a purely theoretical point, can be made use of in a technique of self-therapy.

154: In "The Body in its Sexual Being," Merleau-Ponty considers the "affective life" in regard to its embodiment. According to him, it is Eros which underlies the intentionalities of cognition. Without attraction and aversion, cognitiveness would continue to slumber. Eros awakens and motivates perception, motility, and the organizing of space. (Cf. pp. 263–73 and exercise 30, pp. 258–59.) "Let us try," he says, "to see how a thing or a being begins to exist for us through desire or love and we shall thereby come to understand better how things and beings can exist in general." But, insofar as desire is responsible for the emerging of the subject-object relationship, it is also responsible for the pathological polarizations which make that relationship needlessly painful, a persistent source of frustration, disappointment, and suffering. (See pp. 168–71.)

All we need to do is ask ourselves whether, and to what extent, our relationships with the beings that exist for us are indeed full of love: tender, caring, rejoicing, celebratory. If the love we are *normally* capable of, along with its familiar distortions, impairments, and fixations, can suffice to 'bring into being' what exists for us, just imagine what a deeper, more expansive, more open kind of love would make possible! (See pp. 188–90.) Through a feeling for being that is in touch with itself and free of anxieties, defenses, and fixations, our relationships with persons and things would be significantly more fulfilling: the beings that existed for us would come forth in a more beautiful, more meaningful presence.

156: At the same time that he recognizes the "erotic structure" of human perception, Merleau-Ponty fails to consider the potential for a superior erotic structuring which is implicated by the pathological cases, where he observes that "perception has lost its erotic structure, both spatially and temporally." If *normal* perception can *lose* its erotic energy, can it not also intensify it, and modify the way that energy *structures* the perceptual situation? Vision, for example, can cease to be so lustful, so blind to pain and suffering, so bent on mastering, controlling, and fixing with its stare. The gaze can become more compassionate, more responsive to the visibility of pain and suffering, more kindly; it can become gentle, more radiant of warmth and joy. (See pp. 263–73, 286–87, 137–38, and 145–46, and exercise 15, pp. 94–97.) The erotic structuring *need not* polarize the perceptual situation into a subject-object duality; it can, instead, move toward freedom and openness, a well-balanced relationship. *Time, Space, and Knowledge* works with perception and motility on precisely this level: the level of feeling. For it is *here* that we find the potential for openness—an Eros, a polymorphous libido, that is free of inveterate tendencies to structure relationships in unfortunate ways. (See exercise 17, pp. 172–73, and p. xiii.)

164: "The body can symbolize existence because it brings it into being and actualizes it." Is this not an understanding of embodiment which invites the process of visualization? The symbolic or ideal image of embodiment gradually brings 'a new body' into being, like a work of art. "The body is to be compared," Merleau-Ponty says, "not to a physical object, but rather to a work of art" (*PP*, p. 150). In context, he means mainly to stress the organic unity of the conscious body in contrast to the very different unity of physical objects. But it is precisely this difference, after all, which makes the metamorphoses discussed in *Time, Space, and Knowledge* possible.

Visualizations show that the body is like a work of art in another sense, too. When Merleau-Ponty writes, then, that "the body is solidified or generalized existence, and existence a perpetual incarnation" (*PP*, p. 166), we are to understand (i) that the body is a condensation, a reduction, a local expression and enfolding of existence, but (ii) that, in the very nature of things, the body is always undergoing a process of unfolding, of transformation. Thus, the question at stake is only whether or not this "perceptual incarnation" will be welcomed, accepted, and responsibly worked with. How we respond to the fact of impermanence, the fact of "perpetual reincarnation," is a matter of the utmost importance for our well-being, our vitality, and our power to make something supremely meaningful of existence.

Consistent with the *Abhidharma* tradition, as developed through the *Vajrayana, Time, Space, and Knowledge* discloses the fact that there is "a more general drama which arises from the metaphysical structure of my body" (*PP*, p. 167); and it teaches us how to become more appreciatively and openly attuned to this more general drama.

209: Here begins a lengthy discussion of the human experiencing of color. (Color is discussed elsewhere in *PP* on pp. 153, 209–14, 227–29, 234, and 304–13.) What is the significance of the fact that we see the world as colored, or colorful? We commonly recognize that our feelings, emotions, and moods color the world perceived. We also easily recognize the influence of colors, of luminosity, of the atmosphere of light, on our states of mind.

The *Tibetan Book of the Dead*[5] makes use of ancient wisdom concerning the relationship between qualities of illumination and modes of awareness. It suggests that this wisdom can be therapeutic. The *Vajrayana* is likewise attentive to the symbolic, healing values inherent in light and its colors. Despite its modernity, *Time, Space, and Knowledge* also works with our experience of light. (See, for example, exercise 17, p. 172, and exercise 32, pp. 271–73.) Attunement to vibrations and halos of light can significantly alter one's experience of space and spatial relationships.

Merleau-Ponty's discussion can contribute much, I think, toward our understanding of these elusive matters. For example, it suggests the possibility that a more "sympathetic relation" with colors, a gaze more responsive, perhaps, to the luminous radiations of things, really could help us to dissolve, or at least soften, the subject-object polarization which fixates, objectifies, distances, and thus dims down, the things we behold. (See *PP*, pp. 214 and 227.) For: "In reality, each colour, in its inmost depths, is nothing but the inner structure of the thing overtly revealed" (*PP*, p. 229).

According to Merleau-Ponty, vision is the realizing, or actualizing, of a certain potential for the openness of nondualistic relationships: "To say that I have a visual field is to say that by reason of my position I have access to, and an opening upon, a system of beings, that these are at the disposal of my gaze in virtue of a kind of primordial contract and through a gift of nature" (*PP*, p. 216). This contract takes place in the holiest continuum of feeling, where vision and its object are not polarized in unproductive conflict. The radiations and vibrations of color also take place in, and consequently affect, this basic relationship in the stratum of feeling. It thus stands to reason that meditative practices designed to make vision more open to the felt qualities radiating as color could *overcome* the tendency of vision to establish dualistic relationships with things.

214: Discussing our perceptual experience of things, Merleau-Ponty writes:

> If the qualities radiate around them a certain mode of existence, if they have the power to cast a spell and what we called just now a sacramental value, this is because *the sentient subject does not posit them as objects, but enters into a sympathetic relation with them,* makes them his own and finds in them his momentary law.

Compare this with the commentary on the "Object and Its Glow" exercise in *Time, Space, and Knowledge* (pp. 172–73), which is designed, of course, to help us transform the painfully dualistic relationship we normally experience in our perceptual encounter with the things in our world. Needless to say, perhaps, Tarthang Tulku believes that we may actually *experience* our perceptual world in the beautiful way Merleau-Ponty has described, whereas I suspect that Merleau-Ponty regards this "radiation," this "power to cast a spell," and this "sacramental value" as more poetry than reality. Were he to have taken his language as concrete phenomenological truth, and not metaphor, he would, perhaps, have moved in the direction of a therapeutic phenomenological praxis.

219: Merleau-Ponty writes:

> The unity of either the subject or the object is not a real unity, but a presumptive unity on the horizon of experience. We must rediscover, as anterior to the ideas of subject and object, the fact of my subjectivity and the nascent object, that primordial layer at which both things and ideas come into being. (Cf. pp. 32, 124, 126, 127, and 193–202.)

Time, Space, and Knowledge can help us with this "rediscovery." As we touch the ground of experience, the continuum of feeling in which subject and object are united in a fruitful, harmonious relationship (or partnership), we can begin to experience a very different kind of space—spacious, expansive, hospitable, and full of opportunities for marvelous adventures. Once we have 'returned' to the primordial, anonymous, prepersonal feeling-continuum of space, we will know for ourselves the answer to Merleau-Ponty's question about the nature of space: "Is it not of its essence," he asks, "to embrace every being that one can imagine . . .?" (*PP*, p. 288) It is not all that easy to feel the *embrace* of space.

Time, Space, and Knowledge invites us to ask whether or not this essential characteristic of space is realized and actually *embodied* in our own experience. The visualization practices proposed in *Time, Space, and Knowledge* may help us to contact the energies latent within our experience, energies which Merleau-Ponty here calls "the essence" of space as we "experience" it, so that we may release them and achieve a more fulfilling experience, a more effective practice, of this embrace. The "essence" Merleau-Ponty describes is, in fact, *the compassionate and fully opened heart* of our spatial embodiment.

285: In his chapter on space, Merleau-Ponty recognizes the possibility of giving a phenomenological description of mythic space: "There is a mythical space in which directions and positions are determined by the residence in it of great affective entities." But, although he thereby makes explicit the experiential grounding of such space, Merleau-Ponty does not pause to consider the potentially meaningful qualities latent in such an experience of 'lived space'. In *Time, Space, and Knowledge*, however, the possibility of contacting and opening up these latent potentialities, and of allowing, even encouraging, their unfolding, is the key to a profoundly beneficial transformation in our experience of a meaningful human existence, a meaningful world of Being.

The visualizations in *Time, Space, and Knowledge* are intended to create, or bring about, through a practice of the schematizing imagination, a new and much more fulfilling experience of space. We may say, if we like, that this is just an imaginary or mythical space. But that is of no importance, ultimately, from the standpoint of a more fulfilling, more fully opened, and more meaningful experiential capacity. (Cf. pp. 40–46.) Merleau-Ponty does note, after all, a point of contact when he states: "For the augur, right and left are the sources of the lawful and the forbidden, just as for me my right hand and my left are respectively the incarnations of my skill and my awkwardness." Perhaps there is a profound *value*, a value he does not suspect, in the augur's experience of right and left. Perhaps there is a wonderful *truth* in that "mythical" experience. And perhaps it would be *therapeutically very meaningful* to realize, within the abode of our experience, the hidden connectedness of these two seemingly incompatible understandings.

290: For readers of *Time, Space, and Knowledge* Merleau-Ponty's chapter on space will be of incalculable value. In the midst of this chapter, we find a very powerful repudiation of the reductive mentality which, feeling threatened by the openness of the *Time, Space, and Knowledge* vision, will stop at nothing to deny its appeal:

> As long as we allow the existence of dreams, insanity or perception, at least as so many forms of absence of reflection—and how can we not do so if we want to leave some value to the testimony of consciousness, without which no truth is possible?—we have no right to level all experiences

down to a single world, all modalities of existence down to a single consciousness.

Expanding his phenomenological description of mythical experience, Merleau-Ponty declares: "The myth holds the essence *within* the appearance; the mythical phenomenon is not a representation, but a genuine presence." And he adds: "Every 'apparition' (*Erscheinung*) is in this case an incarnation. . . . ." This description is, I think, convincing. But what is so precious in this account is that it gives us the key to understanding just why, and how, such mythic experience can be so very meaningful and satisfying: the "essence" of the experiential encounter *comes forth*, the gift of a genuine *presence*. The fulfilling "essence," or value, is not held at a distance, not aversively deferred or postponed; it is not the mutilated or impoverished experience of an unnecessary defensive duality.

Merleau-Ponty continues:

> Things are taken for the incarnation of what they express, and . . . their human significance is compressed into them and presents itself literally as what they mean. A shadow passing or the creaking of branches have each a meaning; everywhere there are warnings with no one who issues them.

True. But why should this sensibility be abandoned? Is there no *alternative* to the sort of "critical examination" upon which objective thinking (the thinking of science) insists? *Time, Space, and Knowledge* seems to suggest a valuable alternative. This is not, however, a regression to primitive or infantile innocence, but rather a very subtle critical understanding which, rather than suppressing or rejecting this sensibility, raises it, precisely by virtue of its critique, into the openness of an enlightened experiential appreciation of the presencing of 'fictitious being'.

291: In an astonishing passage, easy to overlook, Merleau-Ponty writes:

> What *protects* the *sane man* against delirium or hallucination, is not his critical powers, but *the structure of his space:* objects remain *before* him, keeping their *distance* and . . . touching him only with respect. What brings about both hallucinations and myths is a *shrinkage* in the space directly perceived, *a rooting of things in our body,* the *overwhelming proximity of the object,* the *oneness* of man and the world, which is, not indeed abolished, but *repressed* by everyday perception or by objective thought, and which philosophical consciousness rediscovers. (Italics added.)

We may well doubt whether, or to what extent, there is, today, any recognized philosophical consciousness in the West devoted to the rediscovery—*and adequate articulation*—of the primordial "oneness" which Merleau-Ponty is discussing. But, in any case, I think we may find much that is thought-provoking in this passage. Suppose we begin our interpretation by noting that the notion of "the sane man" is a normative one, relative to a given cultural world. Now, Merleau-Ponty himself characterizes "everyday perception" as "repressive." So, perhaps, "the sane man" is not so sane, not so hale. Perhaps we can imagine a healthier person who would not need to inhabit such repressive modes of perception. Perhaps we can imagine a healthier person who would not need such strong defenses as protection against delirium and hallucination. Indeed, it is even conceivable that the nature of what "the sane man" *calls* "delirium" and "hallucination" is inextricably bound up with the defensiveness and "repression" required to maintain such so-called sanity.

Merleau-Ponty makes an important contribution to our understanding of sanity and madness when he helps us to see, in effect, that these norms of health are constitutive of, and embedded within, the very structure of a personal space. We may then notice that his characterization of that structure coincides precisely with Heidegger's characterization of 'representational experiencing': "objects remain before him, keeping their distance," as indeed they must when encountered within the dualistic framework (*Ge-stell*) of re-presentation (*Vor-stellung*). The distance is not only spatial; as postponement, it is temporal as well. And it is a symptom of defensiveness, postures of aversion, and a never-ending cycle of perceptual and emotional frustration.

Merleau-Ponty says that what brings about both hallucinations and myths is a "shrinkage" in the space directly perceived and "the overwhelming proximity" of the object. However, it must be recalled here that we are no longer speaking from an 'objective' standpoint, but rather from a standpoint which is faithfully 'neutralized' and phenomenological. So we must at least consider the possibility that there are *two very different experiences* of what has been called "shrinkage" and "proximity." What brings about hallucination might well be the "paranoid" sense that such proximity is threatening, scary, beyond one's power to cope. This proximity, however, and the "shrinkage" of space it entails, might also be experienced with a *mythic* sense that such a spatial structure manifests the *presencing* of protective, motherly beings: the "proximity of objects" would thus signify the basically friendly coming-forth of Nature, continually reaffirming its warmth, familiarity, and nurturance. Correspondingly, the "shrinkage" of space might be another way of experiencing what Tarthang Tulku calls, in *Time, Space, and Knowledge,* the "intimacy" of space. And, indeed, Merleau-Ponty notes that "the oneness of man and the world," which everyday perception "represses," may bring about *either* hallucination *or* myth. Depending on what? That is the question Merleau-Ponty neither asks nor answers.

Perhaps we may begin to articulate an answer by observing that, in the one case, the process of perceptual structuring is experienced as painful and yet hard to escape from, whereas, in the other case, the structuring is joyful and deeply fulfilling. This consideration may at least enable us to take more seriously the space and time practices presented in *Time, Space, and Knowledge.* Now, Merleau-Ponty's reference, in this regard, to the experience he describes as "a rooting of things in our body" is quite intriguing. Like the other experiential meanings he discusses in the passage cited, this one is also two-faced. To experience "a rooting of things in our body" *may* express the fact that the world one is facing seizes the body in a very scary, very menacing way. Or, on the other hand, it may express the fact that the world one faces is a familiar world, a kindred world, a world whose flesh is, happily, the *same* as one's own. This sense of rootedness can belong to a very wonderful, ecstatic awareness. It can be the expression of an entirely different, and quite wonderful, mode of incarnation. This, too, may encourage us to take more seriously meditation practices centered around the multidimensional experiencing of our embodiment.

314: Merleau-Ponty speaks here of "a global bodily knowledge which systematically embraces all its parts." Perhaps, though, we could give Merleau-Ponty's choice of the word *embrace* a more concretely truthful, a more profoundly meaningful interpretation, in keeping with Tarthang Tulku's vision. For example, we might ponder how such bodily 'knowledge' could be more warmly, more lovingly, and more self-acceptingly *embodied* in, and experienced as, an "embrace." Perhaps an appropriate visualization practice could help us to embody our own bodily knowledge more fully and with deeper fulfillment, and indeed in a way that would significantly modify, not merely our abstract self-understanding, but even, and most especially, our gestures, our facial responsiveness and expressiveness, our postures, and our skillful activities.

Similarly, we might take more seriously, and more practically, too, Merleau-Ponty's statement that "all tactile perception, while opening itself to an objective 'property', includes a bodily component . . ." (*PP*, p. 315). Again, inspired by the *Time, Space, and Knowledge* approach, which is rigorously experiential, we might well ponder the nature of this tactile 'openness', and even, beyond this, attempt to develop it, to embody it more completely, through the discipline of experiential practice. The holistic approach of *Time, Space, and Knowledge* is intended as a response to our need for guidance, both on the level of abstract understanding and on the level of practice aimed at a *concrete embodiment* of our understanding.

320: All the practices in *Time, Space, and Knowledge* attempt in one way or another to help us break down, or break through, the defenses which we have, in effect, constructed, and which confine us within the painful or deadening limitations of unnecessary experiential dualities. Showing us the very first experiential steps on the way to this breakthrough, Merleau-Ponty writes:

> The thing is inseparable from a person perceiving it, and can never be actually *in itself* because its articulations are those of our very existence, and because it stands at the other end of our gaze or at the terminus of a sensory exploration which invests it with humanity. *To this extent, every perception is a communication or a communion,* . . . or, on the other hand, the complete expression outside ourselves of our perceptual powers and *a coition, so to speak, of our body with things.* (Italics added. Cf. chap. 6, pp. 117–32.)

Now, in what sense is Merleau-Ponty giving us an accurate, truthful phenomenological articulation? He certainly is ready to concede that what he is describing has not been, and *will not be,* immediately *obvious* to everyone. Thus there is a sense in which his phenomenology is true, or faithful, only for those persons who have already resolved to deviate from the inauthentic perceptual norm by infusing their 'simply lived' experience with the penetrating light of phenomenological reflection. Reflection undoubtedly *changes* the experience reflected upon. And yet, it does not seem to Merleau-Ponty that these changes are experientially unmotivated. On the contrary, the new understanding presents itself as, and feels itself to be, a deeper understanding, a true and more faithful understanding, lifting out and making explicit a gift in our experience which would otherwise remain latent, implicit, and unacknowledged. So he astutely defends the truth of his description by noting: "The fact that this may not have been realized earlier is explained by the fact that any coming to awareness of the perceptual world was hampered by the prejudices arising from objective thinking." (See pp. 193–94 and p. 303.)

323: "Each fragment of a visible spectacle satisfies an infinite number of conditions, and it is of the nature of the real to compress into each of its instants an infinity of relations." This, I think, is true. But how well, or how fully, do we realize its truth? To realize the compression, realize it deeply and clearly, is also to realize the potential for a more expansive, more spacious experience of "the real." What can we do to *open up* the space of reality? The answer we find in *Time, Space, and Knowledge* involves us in processes that work according to principles that the *Phenomenology of Perception* helps us to understand. Thus, for example, it is possible to facilitate an experience more

open to time and space by visualizing ourselves at a time
or place different from our normal ones, and then moving there and back, to and fro, with increasing agility and
a progressively deeper *feeling* for the spatio-temporal
field which unites them.

As we 'travel' outward in our centrifugal vision along
more and more of these relational trajectories, we will
begin to cultivate a feeling *for the larger continuum* in
which these time-places exist. This feeling is the basis for a
progressively deepening experience of spatial and temporal infinity—and perhaps the experience of an openness
that even encompasses what is called "infinity" and "eternity."

329: "For it is reflection which objectifies points of view
or perspectives, whereas when I perceive, I belong,
through my point of view, *to the world as a whole*." (Italics
added. Cf. pp. 286–90.) The meditation practices are intended to remind us of our link to the world as a whole by
means of a 'return' to the basic and original dimensions of
our experience: dimensions which are prereflective, even
prepersonal, and prior to the objectifications which normally arise as a matter of course. Such practices are *not at
all* meant to deny the value of reflection, nor are they
meant to annul our objectifications. They are meant, rather, to unfreeze, to warm up, our underlying experiential
process, to release it from unnecessary and unsatisfying
blockages of energy. Ultimately, such practices *root* our
conceptualizations in the dynamic, dramatic unfolding
of our embodiment, thus allowing a much more fruitful

dialogue (Great Knowledge) between the 'dreams' of our original prereflective processes and their reflectively founded objectifications.

347: Discussing what he calls "my anonymous life" (the prepersonal realm, including prenatal existence, which both is and is not 'my own'), Merleau-Ponty writes:

> In order to have some inkling of *the nature of that amorphous existence which preceded my own history*, and which will bring it to a close, I have only to *look within me* at *that time which pursues its own independent course*, and which my personal life utilizes but does not entirely overlay. Because *I am borne into personal existence by a time which I do not constitute*, all my perceptions *stand out against a background* of nature." (Italics added.)

And to this he joins the equally fascinating thought that "the natural object is the *track* left by *this generalized existence*." (Italics added.) Let us consider these points in turn.

Merleau-Ponty's notion of our anonymous, amorphous existence is very close to the non-egological thrust of the Buddhist doctrine of the *skandhas*. What we are wont to call 'consciousness' is merely, from an 'ultimate' standpoint, a transitory 'collection' or 'gathering'. According to Merleau-Ponty, if I "look within me," focusing, that is, on the arising and passing away of the "intentional phases" of my experience, then I will discover "that time which pursues its own independent course. . . ." Now, the meditative practices recommended in *Time, Space, and Knowledge* can be quite helpful in preparing us to experience much, much more than 'some inkling' of the true nature of this amorphous, prepersonal existence. In fact, they can show us the way into a rich, articulate, and very deeply convincing *experience* of that insight which Merleau-Ponty rather summarily describes when he says that "I am borne into personal existence by a time which I do not constitute . . ." The meditations in *Time, Space, and Knowledge* will help us to understand this in a way that deeply penetrates the temporal partitions we have defensively constructed, so that we may actually experience that embracing *whole* of time 'in which' I am born and to which, with my death, I 'return'. This is the experience of transcendence, of an unfolding which opens out into the vastness of time and within which I dwell, a temporal configuration capable of experiencing itself either in ecstatic communion or painful disintegration.

Merleau-Ponty's second remark is surprisingly close to the experiential interpretation of objectivity which we find in *Time, Space, and Knowledge*. When we are able to 'track' more of time and so acquire an experiential grasp of the constituting of appearance, *Time, Space, and Knowledge* tells us we will find that the so-called natural object and the expressive concentration of the percipient subject are simultaneously coemergent. Subject and object are coemergent in, and as, a certain transitory phase in the process of dualistic structuring that brings into being a world of meaning and its world-horizons. Ultimately, even the 'natural object' is, as it were, just a trace, a shadow, a reflection. As Longchenpa, an accomplished fourteenth century Tibetan master, says, it is neither something substantial, nor yet a mere nothing: it is, in brief, the wonder of a colorful presence, a transitory gathering of what we experience, through our senses, as "a natural object, made up of colours, tactile and auditory qualities" (*PP*, p. 347). Thus, what we call the "thing" is an attractive, endlessly fascinating focal point for the concentration of colorful, vibrant, resonant energy.

Do we normally appreciate the things we encounter in this way? Would we like to? *Time, Space, and Knowledge* invites us to practice meditations which may help us to heighten, or intensify, our perceptual life by putting us in touch with the basic energies of awareness that 'underlie' this life. These primordial energies begin to awaken in, and as, our 'normal' perceptual processes, and continue to function—to vibrate and resound—even when we are least attentive. But these energies are potentially much more intense, much more alive, and much more profoundly meaningful than the 'qualities' of our 'normal' perceptual situation, experienced as the duality of subject and object, would lead us to believe. Merleau-Ponty's phenomenological descriptions are true, then. But they are true paradoxically; true, that is, only insofar as we understand them as the precious gifts of skillful phenomenological reflection—as the rare fruits, if you will, of a process of meditation whereby we patiently awaken slumbering reserves of energy and explicitly raise them into the gentle lighting of an intensely appreciative, and very articulate, focal awareness.

351: Acknowledging that what he is supposedly "describing" can be phenomenologically true, even in the face of the fact that most human percipients, including the historical community of philosophers, do *not* experience their perceptual situation as Merleau-Ponty "faithfully" renders it, Merleau-Ponty concedes that "this involves a profound transformation of the notions of body and consciousness." Thus, his explication is really an interpretation whose phenomenological truth essentially *depends* upon the power of his interpretation to *bring about* a transformation which embodies, and thereby *makes true,* the account he gives us. In a sense, Merleau-Ponty's phenomenology is only *potentially true*м*true if we learn and embody what it teaches. So he adds:*

> *As far as the body is concerned, even the body of another, we must learn* to distinguish it from the objective body as set forth in works on physiology. This is not the body which is capable of being inhabited by a consciousness. . . . It is simply a question of recognizing that *the body,* as a chemical structure or an agglomeration of tissues, *is formed, by a process of impoverishment, from a primordial phenomenon of the body-for-us, the body of human experience or the perceived body.* . . . (Italics added.)

This is precisely the point where Tarthang Tulku, essentially in agreement with Merleau-Ponty's characterization of the "process of impoverishment," introduces meditation practices intended to educate, or develop, the experiential body and bring about therapeutically meaningful changes. Of course, it should be kept in mind that his approach is much bolder and much more visionary than Merleau-Ponty's. For Tarthang Tulku, this process of impoverishment is not confined to the ordinary worldly concerns of normal perception, but is part of a much vaster drama—a drama with truly cosmic dimensions. For the 'primordial body' which Merleau-Ponty evokes is really one with the "Body of Knowledge" (see pp. 286–87), whose unfolding has neither beginning nor end.

If we listen with an open mind, we can almost hear Merleau-Ponty saying this himself: "When I turn toward perception, and pass from direct perception to thinking about that perception, I re-enact it, and *find at work in my organs of perception a thought older than myself of which those organs are merely a trace.*" (Italics added.) Do we simply *find* this archaic thought already at work in our organs? Or do we find it, rather, only when we have thoughtfully accepted and embraced our embodiment, and willingly devoted our thought to the being of these organs, giving to them such wisdom as transmutes them, opens them, and empowers them to become the adequate and glorious organs of thought?

420: Under the influence of Heidegger's work on time, Merleau-Ponty writes: "Each present reasserts *the presence of the whole past* which it supplants and anticipates that of *all that is to come,*" so that "the present is *not shut up* within itself but transcends itself towards a future and a past." (Italics added.) This is, for reflection, just good phenomenology. But how many of us actually live our lives with a strong, concrete sense that the present is the harvest of the past and the sowing of the future? How many of us live our lives with a concentration, a focus, on the present that allows it to grant us the fullness, the wholeness, and the ecstasy of its presence? How many of us enjoy 'presence of mind'? How often do we feel "shut up" within the present? How often do we, in effect, completely *miss* the present, the *gift* of the present, being caught up in an imaginary future or a repetition of the past? These are only a few of the questions which will show us, if we answer them honestly, how very frustrating and unfulfilling our normal experience of temporality really is. Merleau-Ponty's description points, once again, in the *direction* of a truth that will not fully convince us until, or unless, we take it to heart and *make it true*. With the help of *Time, Space, and Knowledge,* however, we may begin to realize, even in the course of our daily lives, the present of ecstatic temporality which Merleau-Ponty has well described. (See pp. 120–22, 125–27, and 142.)

421: Merleau-Ponty writes: "The past, therefore, *is* not past, nor the future future. It exists only when a subjectivity is there to *disrupt the plenitude* of being in itself, to adumbrate a perspective, and introduce non-being into it. A past and a future spring forth *when I reach out* towards them." (Italics added. Cf. pp. 125–26.) And he summons up the power of his vision by saying: "I am myself time, a time which 'abides' and does not 'flow' or 'change'." And, in defense, he comments: "This idea . . . is [even] perceived by common sense in its [own] way." In fact, "when we consider our common-sensical understanding, we find that Time is even personified. Everyone thinks that there is here a single, concrete being, *wholly present* in each of its manifestations, as is a man in each of his spoken words." (Italics added.) But Merleau-Ponty emphasizes that "this intuition of time's permanence . . . is *jeopardized by the action of common sense, which thematizes or objectifies it*, which is the surest way of losing sight of it." (*PP,* pp. 421–22. Italics added.)

Returning, now, to our first quotation, we should consider the possibility that there may be different ways for "subjectivity" to "disrupt the plenitude of being." It is certainly true that the *ecstatic* (i.e., vectorial) upsurge of subjectivity is responsible for the partitioning of time, and that this partitioning is normally experienced as a disruption. But is it not conceivable that, by a change in our attitude, a change in our affective relationship to past and future, we could regain that plenitude, experiencing in, and as, the gift of the present the uninterrupted wholeness of time? And, if it be true that "a past and a future spring forth when I reach out towards them," perhaps it may also be true that the *manner* in which I reach out could have a decisive bearing on the experiential characteristics of this past and future. Impatience, willfulness, distraction, perpetual discontent, nostalgia, anxiety, a compulsion to repeat the painfulness of the past, escape into daydreams, and wild utopian thinking—these are some of the many attitudes towards the passage of time which ensure that the plenitude of the present will not be recognized and enjoyed.

Suppose we say, then, that I am a time which "abides." But what does this mean? The present of time is an abode only if I am at ease, at peace with myself and my world; it is an abode only if I know how to abide. (Abiding is what Heidegger calls "dwelling.") When I know how to abide, I am ecstatically present in (with) the present, willingly opened to receiving and accepting it as a precious gift— whatever it may bring forth, in fact. Of course, time continues to pass, to flow and change. But I do not cling to what has passed, whether it be something painful that I feel compelled to repeat or something pleasant that I try to possess. I do not escape the unsatisfactoriness of the moment by dreaming of future victories, or future satisfaction. Nor, finally, do I turn away from the precious gift of the present by vainly imagining something better; instead, I abide by opening up to it, accepting its passage, its flow and change, its constant impermanence. And when I have learned to accept and receive it gratefully, I may be granted the most precious gift of all—the wonderful, abiding presence of the whole of time. (See pp. 142–43 and 183–84.) Merleau-Ponty speaks the truth, then, when he recognizes that to objectify and fixate time, to obstruct its passing presence with temporal partitions, is to lose the abiding meaningfulness of the present.

422: On the nature of time, Merleau-Ponty espouses a position which is, on a certain level of interpretation, very similar to the analysis developed in *Time, Space, and Knowledge*:

> We are not saying that time is *for* someone, which would once more be a case of arraying it out, and immobilizing it. We are saying that time *is* someone, or that temporal dimensions, in so far as they perpetually overlap, bear each other out and ever confine themselves to making explicit what was implied in each, being collectively expressive of that one single explosion or thrust which is subjectivity itself. We must understand time as the subject and the subject as time.

As such, the subject who experiences the temporal *ecstasis* (vectorial nature) of his existence as ecstasy, rather than as agony, is one for whom, as Merleau-Ponty puts it, "to be at present is to be always and forever." But we must be careful to avoid cheap superstition. So Merleau-Ponty warns us, with proper urgency, against what he calls "the illusion of eternity" (*PP*, p. 424). He asks: Are we "coming back in this way to a kind of eternity"? He is wise to call attention to the dangers, or follies, in simpleminded wishful thinking.

423: Merleau-Ponty elucidates his concern, arguing: "The feeling for eternity is a hypocritical one, for eternity feeds on time. . . . Eternity is the time that belongs to dreaming . . . ." And then he poses a question: "Of what nature, then, is that waking time in which eternity takes root? It is the field of presence, in the wide sense, with its double horizon or primary past and future, and *the infinite openness of those fields of presence* that have slid by, or are still possible." (Italics added.) Our notion of Eternity is, then, a fixation, another objectification, another *inauthentic* relationship to "the infinite openness of those fields of presence." Our notion forecloses, or blocks off, this openness.

So much is what we may learn from Nagarjuna's *Mulamadhyamakakarika*. But an *intellectual* understanding is not the same as an *experiential* realization of meaning. *Time, Space, and Knowledge* provides just such an experiential rooting for the conclusion to which Nagarjuna's logic guides us. Thus, nonduality (*shunyata*) of conceptualization is cultivated and clarified in (and as) the *experience* of infinite openness. With regard for the whole of time, such experience involves a transformation of certain basically destructive attitudes, commonly manifest in our way, or 'style' of temporalizing our existence. Among other things, we need to consider here our anxiety over death, tendencies toward absent-mindedness, the compulsive nature of our distractions, our nostalgic hold on the past, the dullness of our normal situational presence, and the extent to which our expectations interfere with the freshness, the spontaneity, and the appropriateness of our existential responsiveness.

430: Merleau-Ponty's analysis of time "discloses subject and object as two abstract 'moments' of a unique structure which is presence." This "unique structure" is the structure of 'timing': both subject and object arise *simultaneously and interdependently*, in a process of differentiation which 'places', or 'positions', them at a spatio-temporal distance from one another. (Cf. pp. 170–73.) This distance may be construed, from the standpoint of desires and needs, as the frustrating circumstance of their postponement. Now, the meditative exercises in *Time, Space, and Knowledge* are very interesting in this regard, since they help us to *experience* the abstractness and, speaking more generally, the unsatisfactoriness inherent in the subject-object duality. When the frustrating nature of such duality is intensely experienced in this way, there is strong motivation for change—and adequate guidance for change will come forth, spontaneously, from within the experiential process itself.

Notes

1. Maurice Merleau-Ponty, *Phenomenology of Perception*, trans. Colin Smith (New York: Humanities Press, 1962). The numbers which begin each commentary unit refer to pages in

this text. (In parenthetical page references, this work is cited as *PP*.)

2. Tarthang Tulku, *Time, Space, and Knowledge: A New Vision of Reality* (Emeryville, Calif.: Dharma Publishing, 1977).

3. Mikel Dufrenne, *The Phenomenology of Aesthetic Experience*, trans. Edward S. Casey and Albert A. Anderson, Studies in Phenomenology and Existential Philosophy (Evanston: Northwestern University Press, 1974).

4. Maurice Merleau-Ponty, *The Primacy of Perception*, trans. William Cobb et al., and ed. James M. Edie, Studies in Phenomenology and Existential Philosophy (Evanston: Northwestern University Press, 1964).

5. W. Y. Evans-Wentz, ed., *Tibetan Book of the Dead* (Oxford: Oxford University Press, 1960).

CHAPTER 7

Nothing seems more obvious than that human beings have bodies and minds, and that the two are somehow related. Yet, so far, every attempt to explicate this relationship has run into difficulties of one sort or another. James White, in the article that follows, discusses the mind-body problem in general, outlines some traditional approaches to it, and points out the shortcomings of each.

How do we account for this failure, on the part of philosophers and scientists alike, to uncover the connection between body and mind? Dr. White traces the difficulties to certain inaccurate views of what it is that needs connecting. Ordinarily, the human body is considered to be a discrete entity, separated from other objects by well-defined boundaries. And the mind, too, is generally treated as an object, though an immaterial one, with special functions; this mind accompanies the body on its wanderings through ordinary space. Dr. White, however, suggests that this representation, in itself, makes the mind-body problem insoluble.

Time, Space, and Knowledge offers an alternative, which Dr. White calls the "open 'space' perspective." From this standpoint, objects are presentations of space by time. The barriers that appear to separate one thing from another are themselves seen to be space, so that they are 'present' without compromising the unity of Being. The mind, on the other hand, is likened to the viewing aperture on a camera; it is merely a specific focus on space, and not a 'thing' at all.

Examined from the open 'space' perspective, then, the mind-body problem simply dissolves. What 'there is' is just 'space' made manifest by 'time' in the ways allowed by a particular 'focal setting', which is not, in itself, anything distinct from time and space. So from one point of view, 'mind' and 'body' turn out to be so thoroughly connected that no analysis could ever get them apart to examine their relationship; while from another, the question of their connection is an empty one. For only 'things' can be connected, and mind and body are not 'things'.

Readers interested in the mind-body problem should also see A. Foster's article, and chapters 1, 2, 3, and 9 of *Time, Space, and Knowledge*. Related issues are also discussed by D. Beere, K. Puhakka, R. Puligandla, and R. Romanyshyn.

James E. White

TIME, SPACE, AND KNOWLEDGE
and the Mind-Body Problem

I n science, as well as in everyday life, it is customary to distinguish between the mental and the physical. The former category includes such objects, states, and activities as afterimages and thoughts, happiness and depression, and visualizing and remembering. The category of the physical also includes objects, states, and activities: tables and electrons, solidity and liquidity, and the movement of things through space.

Just as the distinction between these two classes of phenomena seems obvious, so does their interconnection. Yet, when the matter is investigated more closely, problems arise almost immediately. How are mental states related to brain processes? What features do mental items have that physical ones do not? And so on. Each of these issues, in turn, bears on the more general question of how the mental is related to the physical, a question that is known as the *mind-body problem*.

Determining the attributes that characterize the mental and the physical seems as if it might shed important light on the mind-body problem. For if mental items have the same properties as physical ones, then perhaps there is no special difficulty about their relationship. So, before going further, let us consider two features of mental items that tradition has picked out as being particularly important. First, there is *consciousness*. Mental objects exist only as objects *of* consciousness; the notion of a mental object apart from consciousness is absurd. Mental events, too, seem to involve consciousness in an essential way. Second, there is *intentionality*, the referring quality or 'aboutness' of mental states and events. Dreaming, hoping, fearing, and thinking are always specified or identified in terms of what they are *about*; and likewise, dreams, hopes, fears, and thoughts always *refer* to something, whether it is past, present, or future, actual or possible.

Are consciousness and intentionality equally essential in the physical realm? It is hard to see that they are. Physical events can occur when nobody is conscious of them, and these events do not have to be about anything. It appears, then, that the mental and physical are really two logically distinct categories, involving items that have dif-ferent properties. Thus, the problem of their relation seems, at least on the surface, to be a genuine one.

Some Traditional Approaches

Philosophers who have struggled with the mind-body problem fall into two main camps. Members of the one group, which includes Plato and Descartes, contend that the mental is not identical with the physical, that these two irreducible categories contain fundamentally differ-ent sorts of existents. This metaphysical view is called *dualism*. As might be expected, dualists are primarily concerned with the exact relation between the mental and physical, and of course they have not always agreed with one another. For example, Descartes argued that there is a causal relation that works both ways: mental happenings cause physical ones, and vice versa. However, Leibniz denied this and maintained instead that there is a "pre-established harmony" between mental and physical events which resembles the coordinated ticking of two perfectly synchronized clocks.

The other main group of philosophers includes those who hold, despite the differences noted above, that there is some kind of identity relation between the mental and physical. *Materialists* believe that mental items reduce to physical ones, that what we call "mental" is really something physical (e.g., behavior or brain processes). For *idealists*, the reduction goes the other way: physical items are reduced to mental ones, so that what we call "physical" is considered to be, in reality, something mental. An idealist might say that so-called physical objects such as tables are really just collections of sensory impressions or ideas. A third alternative, expressed in Spinoza's *double-aspect theory*, is that the mental and physical are aspects of the same underlying reality.

Generally speaking, dualism has not found favor among modern philosophers. One persuasive criticism, made by Gilbert Ryle in his *Concept of Mind*, is that in lumping the mental and the physical together into the category of substantial things, dualism makes a "category mistake."[1] This, according to Ryle's account, is like saying that a university is the same sort of thing as the campus buildings. Another commonly heard complaint is that dualism conflicts with *Ockham's Razor*, the methodological principle that one ought not to multiply entities beyond necessity. Those who argue this way generally assume that science will be able to explain everything in terms of physical objects and processes, so that references to the mental will become unnecessary.

That, then, leaves only the *monistic* theories, those that hold there is an identity relation between the mental and physical. The trouble with these theories is that the various identities they postulate do not seem to hold in all cases. The materialist who tries to reduce all mental items to physical ones has trouble with mental objects such as afterimages. For example, in closed-eye vision an afterimage has a definite color and shape, and these phenomenal qualities do not seem to be properties of anything physical. Nor is the blue color of a cloudless sky a property of any physical object. The idealist has similar difficulties in trying to reduce physical properties such as mass, volume, and location to something mental. What mental items have these physical properties? And as for the double-aspect theory, it leaves unexplained the mysterious underlying reality that has both mental and physical aspects.

Perhaps *Time, Space, and Knowledge* can give us some insights into the mental and physical that are not provided by the standard philosophical theories, and since its insights are grounded in meditative experience, they may also prove more satisfactory than those that have been offered to date.[2] Before turning to the *Time, Space, and*

Knowledge vision, however, it will be instructive to see how Descartes generated and responded to the mind-body problem; the value of the Time-Space-Knowledge vision shows itself more clearly when it is contrasted with Descartes's classical dualism. For similar reasons, it will be useful to briefly compare the *Time, Space, and Knowledge* view of mind with that of another important philosopher, Immanuel Kant.

Descartes, Kant, and
TIME, SPACE, AND KNOWLEDGE

Descartes begins his *Meditations* by subjecting all his beliefs to doubt, in the hope of finding a truth that is certain.[3] His famous discovery was that the proposition *I exist* is true and known with certainty whenever I say it or think it, even if I am dreaming or having delusions. It is absolutely indubitable; after all, how can I doubt that I exist without existing? Once this is established, however, the problem of *what* it is that exists, of what *I* am, still remains.

Descartes assumed that the self is a *thing*, or a *substance*, to use the scholastic term. But what sort of thing? The self is not identical with the body, Descartes argued, because it might exist without a body. A person could, for example, be deceived when he thinks he has a body; he might have a purely mental existence without a body; but he cannot exist without being conscious. So Descartes concluded that human existence is *essentially* a thinking existence and that the self is a thinking thing, a *res cogitans*. He still considered this *res cogitans* to be a substance, but an immaterial one, with no physical properties such as extension in space, location, or velocity—rather like the Hindu *atman* or the Christian *soul*.

Continuing his meditations, Descartes found that he also had to grant the reality of the material world and, in particular, the reality of human bodies. So he was confronted with his own version of the mind-body problem: How is the *res cogitans*, the immaterial mind, related to the physical body? His answer was that there is a two-way causal relation. In perception, physical events in the body cause mental events in the immaterial mind. In volition, mental acts of the will produce physical events in the body.

Obviously, it is difficult to explain how this interaction works. Descartes claimed that the pineal gland functions as a kind of way station between the body and the mind, but of course there is no evidence that the pineal gland serves this purpose. In fact, it has proven very difficult to make *any* correlations between cognitive activities such as remembering and imagining and specific brain processes. A further difficulty is that the nature of the causation itself becomes very unclear when cause and effect take place in radically different 'realms'. Finally, there is the problem of self-awareness: How does one discern this immaterial mind? In ordinary introspection, we find no such thing, only fleeting thoughts and mental processes. So how do we determine whether it exists at all? And what happens to the mind during deep and dreamless sleep, for example? If the essence of the immaterial mind is to think, then it must be thinking during deep and dreamless sleep or else cease to exist. But we are never aware of such thinking, so for all we know, the mind 'disappears' during this period.

Let us now turn to the *Time, Space, and Knowledge* vision. Exercises 1–10 encourage a progressive widening of our perspective on the body, until we perceive it as 'space', and not as a solid object with dimensions, location, and an opaque surface. This 'space' can be characterized negatively as *not* being ordinary space, but I am not confident that I can describe it in any positive way. It can, however, be experienced by practicing these exercises.

What of the *Time, Space, and Knowledge* view of the mind? In exercise 11 ("The Source of Thoughts," p. 51),* we are asked to try to discover the origin or source of thoughts, using the 'space' perspective developed in the first ten exercises. When I do this, I find no Cartesian immaterial substance, no *res cogitans*; thoughts just appear and disappear.

Now, I admit that Descartes would not take this failure to find the mind as any evidence that it does not exist. His claim, after all, was that we know the existence of the mind *by inference*: "If I think, then I (an immaterial mind) exist." And he might have gone on to argue that awareness of the mind itself, apart from its thinking, would require being aware of it as a mental object, an object of consciousness. That, to be sure, is an impossibility: the mind is the *subject* that is conscious, not an object of conscious-

---

*This and all of the parenthetical page references that follow are to *Time, Space, and Knowledge.*—Ed.

ness, and trying to be conscious of the mind would be like trying to see your right eye with your right eye.

Yet this reply is not entirely satisfactory. It may be that we cannot see the eye with the eye, but we can experience it in other ways. For instance, we can feel it with our fingers. Similarly, there ought to be some experience (even if it is one that is out of the ordinary) that would confirm or disconfirm the existence of the immaterial mind. Perhaps the more open 'space' perspective developed in the *Time, Space, and Knowledge* vision can provide such an experience. If the perspective is really all-inclusive, in the sense that anything involved in our being is directly knowable and can be traced back to 'space' (see p. 41), then the failure to find the mind from this wider 'space' perspective would, indeed, be conclusive evidence that it does not exist.

The fact that ordinary experience fails to discern a generative source of thoughts cannot, then, provide adequate grounds for denying its existence. The elementary particles of modern physics, after all, cannot be viewed in any ordinary way, and yet we still believe that they exist as constituents of larger things. These particles *are* 'available' to us in the wider 'space' perspective, however, and so is the immaterial mind, if there is one.

But even if we are willing to admit the possibility of there being no 'source' of thoughts, it is no easy matter to give up the notion of something that lies 'behind' and directs our body's doings. It almost seems that we can *experience* the mind functioning as a *causal agent*: I can move my arm at will, and in doing this, it is *me* doing it—a self, mind, or ego. Furthermore, in the context of freedom, moral responsibility, and punishment, we assume that persons *act* and that their actions can be right or wrong, blameworthy or excusable, rewardable or punishable. These distinctions seem to be essential to morality, and yet they, too, presuppose some immaterial agent. We do not reward the hand that pulled the child from danger, nor the nervous system that coordinated its movements, nor anything else that is tangible.

However, from the more open 'space' perspective, moral distinctions appear rigid and arbitrary. Can we really divide actions into rigid categories: mine and yours, right and wrong, punishable or excused? If actions are traced back to 'space', then these distinctions no longer apply. What is involved in the feeling of *me as agent* is, perhaps, the phenomenon of "coming out," discussed in exercise 9 ("Participation as Observer," pp. 36–38). The 'self' emerges from the 'space' experience in order to observe and examine it, and this 'freezes' the experience as *mine*, as something I do. If I could retain the openness of the 'space' perspective, then perhaps I would no longer have this feeling.

But what happens to morality, if moral distinctions no longer apply? It seems that conventional morality would be inappropriate and would have to be replaced by some 'higher morality' emphasizing flexibility, openness, self-lessness, universal compassion, and friendliness. At the very least, I perceive some basis for a more open, flexible morality in the 'space' perspective.

Thus far, I have discussed the Cartesian view of the mind as an immaterial substance causally connected with the body. The rejection of this view in *Time, Space, and Knowledge* is based on the failure to find such a thing in the wider 'space' perspective. But there is another philosophical view of the mind that escapes this attack. The Kantian "transcendental ego" is, by definition, beyond *all* possible experience; it could not be experienced even from the 'space' perspective. It is posited as the basis of the *unity* of our ordinary experience. The ego itself, however, cannot possibly be experienced because the "categories of the understanding" and the "forms of sensibility" do not apply to it. It exists in the so-called *noumenal* realm, the realm of things-in-themselves, and not in the *phenomenal* realm, the realm of experience. Or at least this was Kant's view.

Experience does seem to possess a kind of unity when I grasp it as belonging to me, as mine. But as mentioned above, this involves the "coming out" phenomenon, where I 'fix' the experience as personal and unitary, in order to observe it. If I let go of this tendency, then there is no longer any need to posit a transcendental ego. Then, too, it might be that from the most open 'space' view, involving Great Space, even so-called things-in-themselves could be experienced apart from the usual categories of understanding and forms of sensibility.

So much for philosophical theories. There remains the problem of clarifying the *Time, Space, and Knowledge* vision of the mind.

The TIME, SPACE, AND KNOWLEDGE Vision of Mind

From the more open 'space' perspective, there is no mind, no body, and no thoughts: there is just 'space'. Even the discovery that "everything is 'space '" is itself 'space'. (See p. 42.) But this discovery does not mean that there is no ordinary experience—in ordinary space—of the body, thoughts, the mind, and their interplay. The more open 'space' experience includes these experiences as part of a wider vision. Still, one of the discoveries of the 'space' experience is that there is no mind-as-generative-source—no immaterial substance—and no material substance having an absolute location and dimensions.

To put the point another way, the distinctions that are the basis of Descartes's dualism simply do not apply to our experience, whether it be ordinary experience or that of the more open perspectives. There are no immaterial substances vs. material substances, no mind-as-cause vs. thoughts-as-effects. As Ryle aptly put it, these distinctions reflect the myth of "the ghost in the machine."

The rejection of metaphysical dualism in the *Time, Space, and Knowledge* vision may tempt us to switch to some alternative philosophical theory. For instance, a version of the double-aspect theory may appear attractive, perhaps one that asserted that there is one reality, namely 'space', which is seen as either mental or physical. But attributing a philosophical theory to the *Time, Space, and Knowledge* vision would be a mistake. This vision is not confined to any one theory, viewpoint, or perspective; it is open to different perspectives. Viewing things from the most open of these, the one in which Great Space-Time-Knowledge appears, ordinary concepts or theories are simply inappropriate. Great Space-Time-Knowledge cannot be said to be either one or many, existent or non-existent, nothing or something. It transcends these distinctions.

But if no ordinary concepts or theories apply to Great Knowledge, does this mean that it is *ineffable* in the sense that nothing can be said about it at all? To assert this would be to adopt still another limiting theory, and one that is inaccurate, as well. The *Time, Space, and Knowledge* vision provides many illuminating insights that *can* be communicated, as we have seen, but these do not take the form of philosophical or scientific theories. Instead, the author uses the language of poetry, with its similes, metaphors, and other figurative language. For example, in a very suggestive passage, the mind is said to be like the viewing aperture of a camera:

> The mind is not a palpable or solid thing (except insofar as we take feeling tones and other mental events for the mind). Rather, it is perhaps simplest to say that the mind is a sign of a specific focal setting being taken on Great Space. The mind is like the viewing aperture on a camera. It is a focus on Great Space, being open to it in various ways and degrees that we could call particular focal settings. It is not surprising that this mind is hard to find when we search for it, for how can we locate a 'setting'? (p. 64)

This view of the mind suggests a kind of freedom not allowed by science or even philosophy—the freedom to open the focal setting of the mind to broader 'space' perspectives. This is done by *allowing* the focus to open, by relaxing the mind, and not particularly by doing something. On this view, the mind is not a fixed subject observing from some particular standpoint, but only an arbitrary focal setting that can be changed. Moreover, this focal setting is not itself an object or thing to be experienced. And, when completely opened, even it disappears in the all-encompassing vision that is Great Space-Time-Knowledge.

Notes

1. Gilbert Ryle, *Concept of Mind* (New York: Barnes and Noble, 1949).

2. Tarthang Tulku, *Time, Space, and Knowledge: A New Vision of Reality* (Emeryville, Calif.: Dharma Publishing, 1977).

3. René Descartes, *Meditations*, trans. Lawrence J. Lafleur (Indianapolis: Bobbs-Merrill, 1960).

Contributors

Tarthang Tulku, a Tibetan lama living in Berkeley, California, has taught in the United States for the past decade. He is the author of *Time, Space, and Knowledge*.

Edward S. Casey is presently Professor of Philosophy at the State University of New York at Stony Brook. Dr. Casey studied philosophy at Yale University (B.A., 1961), the University of Paris (Fulbright Fellowship, 1964–66), and Northwestern University (Ph.D., 1967). A translator of two books of Mikel Dufrenne, he has written *Imagining: A Phenomenological Study* (Bloomington, Ind.: Indiana University Press, 1976). He is currently finishing a sequel to *Imagining* to be entitled *Remembering*.

Bill Jackson received B.S. and M.S. degrees in Psychology from Iowa State University and a Ph.D. in Psychology from Purdue University. His varied career includes four years of teaching at the University of Wisconsin at Madison, the practice of clinical psychology at the Madison Psychiatric Associates from 1969 to the present, and the research and authoring of several books and articles including *Afire with Serenity* (Center City, Minn.: Hazelden, 1977).

Kaisa Puhakka, a native of Finland, received both an M.A. in Comparative Philosophy and a Ph.D. in Cognitive Psychology from the University of Toledo. She was a Visiting Lecturer at the University of Helsinki in 1975, taught in the Department of Psychology at Mary Washington College in Virginia (1977–80), and is currently teaching at Adelphi University in New York. Her publications include *Knowledge and Reality: A Comparative Study of Quine and Some Buddhist Logicians* (Delhi: Banarsidass, 1975).

David Michael Levin received his B.A. from Harvard University in 1961, and his Ph.D. in Philosophy from Columbia University in 1967. From 1961–62 he studied at the University of Paris on a Fulbright Fellowship. He taught at the Massachusetts Institute of Technology from 1969–72, and has been a member of the Philosophy Department of Northwestern University since 1972. He has authored *Reason and Evidence in Husserl's Phenomenology* (Evanston, Ill.: Northwestern University Press, 1970) and is currently working on a book entitled *The Education of Embodiment: An Experiential Interpretation of Heidegger.*

Ralph H. Moon received his Ph.D. in Philosophy from Purdue University and is currently teaching at the University of Louisville. He is also a graduate of the 1976 Human Development Training Program, given by Tarthang Tulku at Nyingma Institute in Berkeley, California.

Robert C. Scharff received his A.B. from the University of Illinois in 1961, and his M.A. (1965) and Ph.D. (1970) in Philosophy from Northwestern University. Dr. Scharff taught at the U.S. Air Force Academy (1966–1968) and the University of Oklahoma (1968–1969), and has been a member of the Philosophy Department at the University of New Hampshire since 1970. He is the author of articles on Nietzsche, Dilthey, and Heidegger, including "Heidegger's Path of Thinking and the Way of Meditation in the Early Upanisads" in *The Question of Being: East-West Perspectives* (ed. Mervyn Sprung [University Park, Pa.: Pennsylvania State University Press, 1978]), and is currently working on a book, tentatively entitled *Presence and Reason: Before and After Metaphysics*.

James Shultz attended graduate theological school at the Chicago Theological Seminary and received his Ph.D. in Interdisciplinary Social Sciences from the University of Chicago. Dr. Shultz currently lives with his wife and two children in Berkeley, California, where he is a teacher, lecturer, and consultant. He has been a student of Tarthang Tulku, Rinpoche, for the past eight years.

James E. White received his B.A. from Dartmouth in 1961, and his M.A. and Ph. D. degrees in Philosophy (1968) from the University of Colorado. From 1964 to the present he has been teaching philosophy at St. Cloud University in Minnesota, and has authored a text, *Basic Philosophy* (Minnesota: Palladin Press, 1972), in addition to several articles published in philosophical journals around the world.